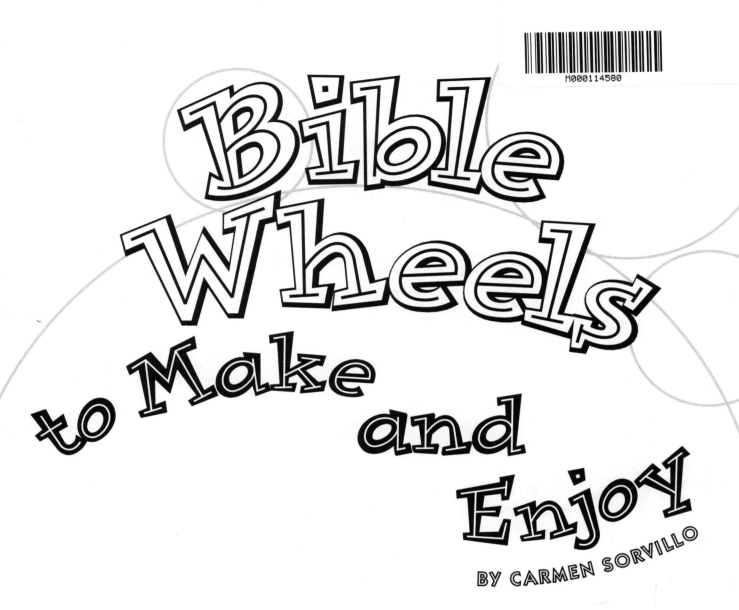

Bible Wheels to Make and Enjoy

BY CARMEN SORVILLO

CPH™
SAINT LOUIS

Published by Concordia Publishing House
3558 S. Jefferson Avenue, St. Louis, MO 63118-3968
Manufactured in the United States of America

1 2 3 4 5 6 7 8 9 10 09 08 06 05 03 02 01 00

Contents

Old Testament

New Testament

(All stories are in the order in which they appear in the Bible.)

Introduction

Bible Wheels to Make and Enjoy is a book of hands-on projects. These manipulative wheels are not meant to replace the way you normally teach Bible stories but to supplement it. They are fun activities that will reinforce what you are teaching and help your students remember the lessons. These *Bible Wheels* are designed for children to create and use with little or no help from an adult. The text is minimal and some wheels are limited to the title of the story and the Bible reference. The cutting is simple enough for most children; however, depending on your time constraints and/or the age and ability level of your students, you or an assistant may wish to do some or all of the cutting before distributing the wheels to the children. The *Bible Wheels* in this book will engage the students on several levels. Not only are they fun to cut out and assemble, but they also mystify children and often elicit a "Wow, how does that work?" reaction.

How to Use This Book

The ways that these wheels can be incorporated into Bible lessons are as varied as the teachers themselves. You may wish to teach your lesson as usual and use the wheels afterward. This will provide at least one more repetition of the story in class and most likely another freely volunteered retelling at home for parents. *Bible Wheels* are also a great take-home activity for children and their parents to do together. You may, instead, wish to use them as a launching activity, to spark students' interest in reading or hearing more about the story. Start by distributing the copies of the wheels, scissors, and crayons. After your students have made the wheel, ask them what they think is happening on the wheel and what they think the day's lesson is about. Then read or teach the full text of the story after the children's interest has been sparked. Making *Bible Wheels* can be a worthwhile emergency activity for a substitute teacher. They can also be used as activities for child care while parents attend meetings or services. Cutting, assembling, and coloring the wheels will pass the time more meaningfully for the children. You will undoubtedly find many more uses for these wheels, based on your own teaching style and your students' needs.

Making the Wheels

The wheels are printed double-sided but should be photocopied onto 8½″ x 11″ paper with the back of each sheet left blank. When photocopying you might want to manually position the page on the copy machine rather than use autofeed. This will insure that the entire outer circle or rectangle is reproduced on the copy.

The easiest way for an adult to cut out the wheel windows is with an arts & crafts knife. Children can poke a hole and then cut with safety scissors. The teacher or assistant might start the cuts for students or even precut the wheels and have the students color them only. Use brass fasteners to secure the two wheels together. They are inexpensive and readily available at office supply stores.

1. The circle or rectangle with the story title is the top section. First cut out the shape along its outline, cut out the windows (✂), and then cut two short intersecting slits at the center.
2. Cut out the bottom circle and cut two short intersecting slits at its center.
3. Place the top section over the bottom circle, line up the center cross-slits, and push a brass fastener through the slits from the top.
4. Carefully turn both pieces over. Separate the two brass flanges and press flat.
5. Turn it right-side up again so that the text is readable and holding the top section with your left hand, make sure the circle below is free to turn.
6. With your right hand turn the bottom circle so that the number 1 along the outer edge lines up with the short line along the edge of the top section.
7. Now turn the bottom wheel downward through the numbered sequence. (There is no numbered order for Noah's Ark.)

CUT ALONG EDGE

Creation

(Genesis 1:1-2:3)

And God blessed the seventh day and made it holy, because on it He rested from all the work of creating that He had done (Genesis 2:3).

Creation

Bottom

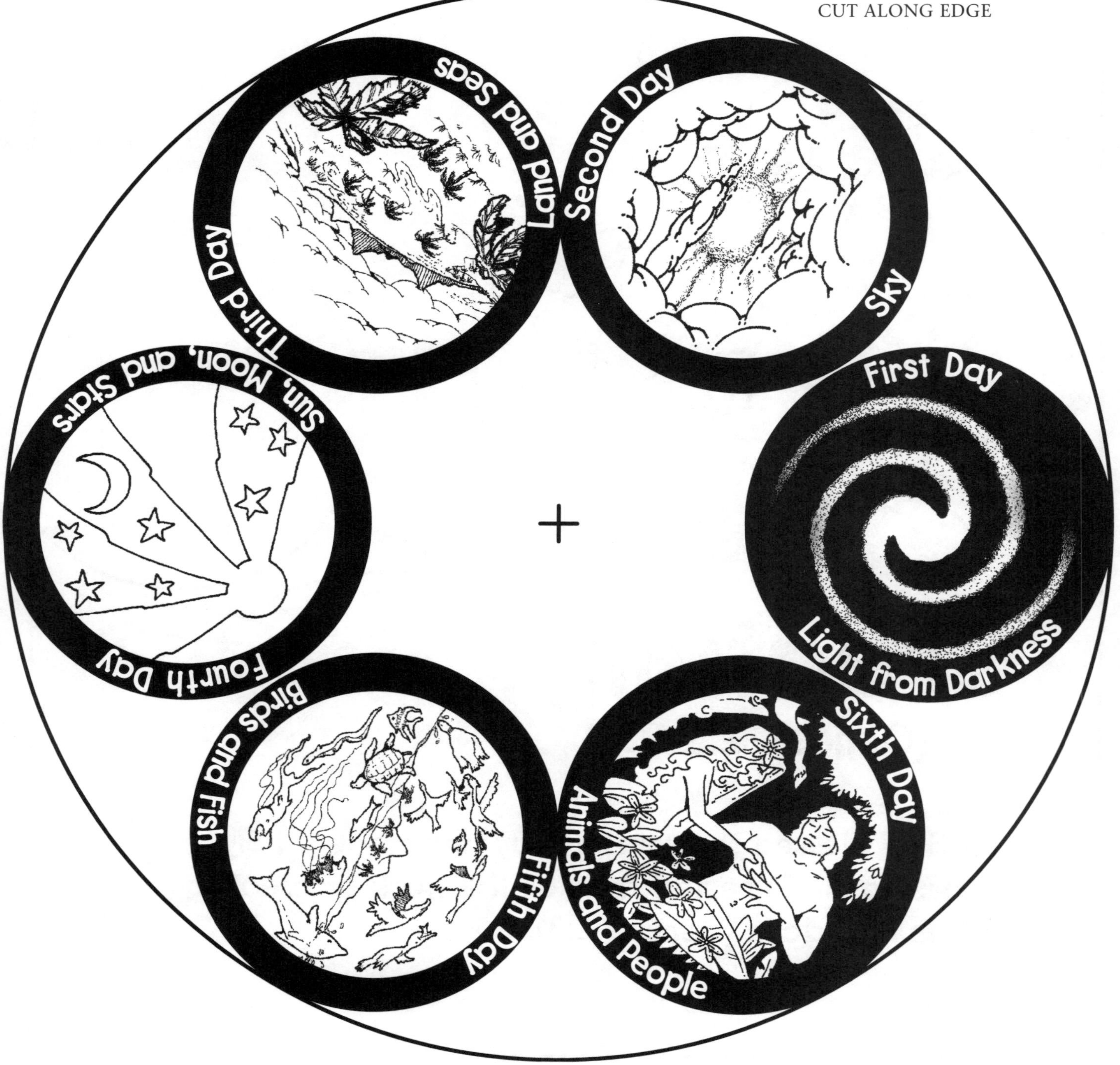
CUT ALONG EDGE
First Day
Light from Darkness
Second Day
Sky
Third Day
Land and Seas
Fourth Day
Sun, Moon, and Stars
Fifth Day
Birds and Fish
Sixth Day
Animals and People

Noah's Ark

Noah's Ark (Genesis 6:1–9:17)
You are to bring into the ark two of all living creatures, male and female, to keep them alive with you (Genesis 6:19).

CUT ALONG THE HEAVY LINE OF THE DOOR NOAH IS HOLDING.

CUT ALONG EDGE

Noah's Ark

Bottom

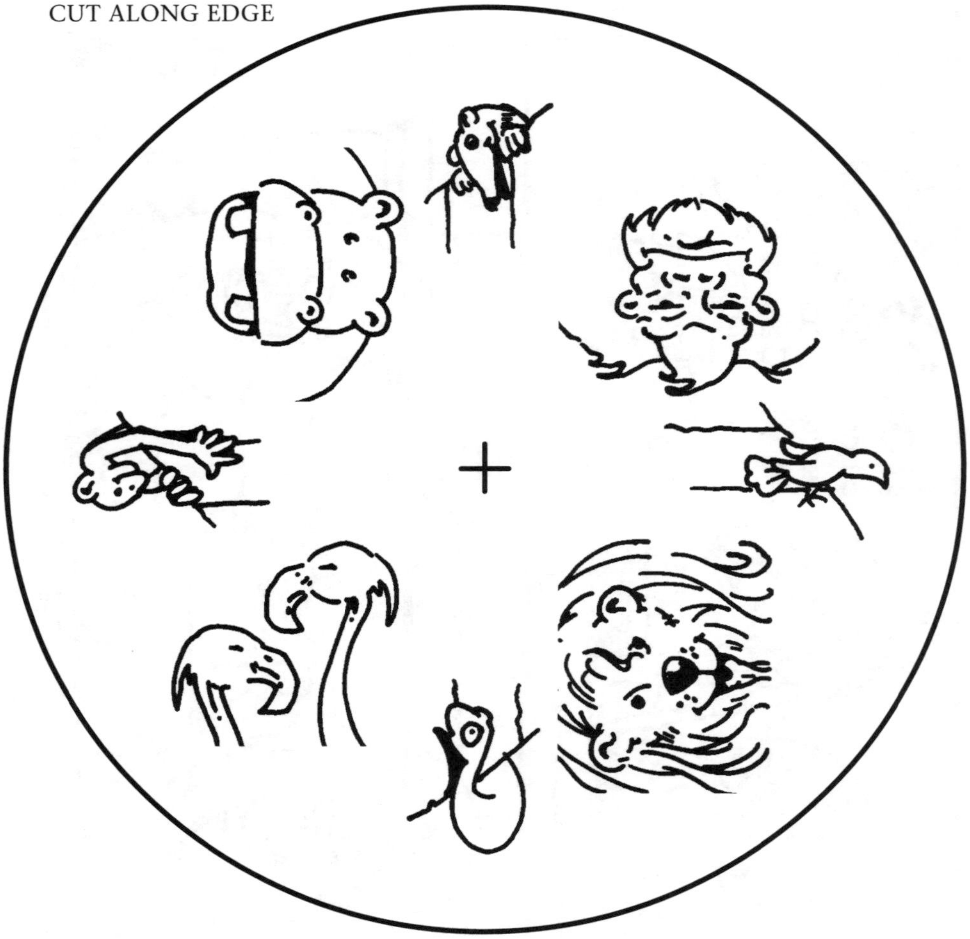
CUT ALONG EDGE

Top

God's Promise to Abraham

God's Promise to Abraham

(Genesis 12:1-9)

The LORD had said to Abraham, "Leave your country,
your people and your father's household
and go to the land I will show you.
I will make you into a great nation
and I will bless you."
(Genesis 12:1-2)

CUT ALONG EDGE

God's Promise to Abraham

Bottom

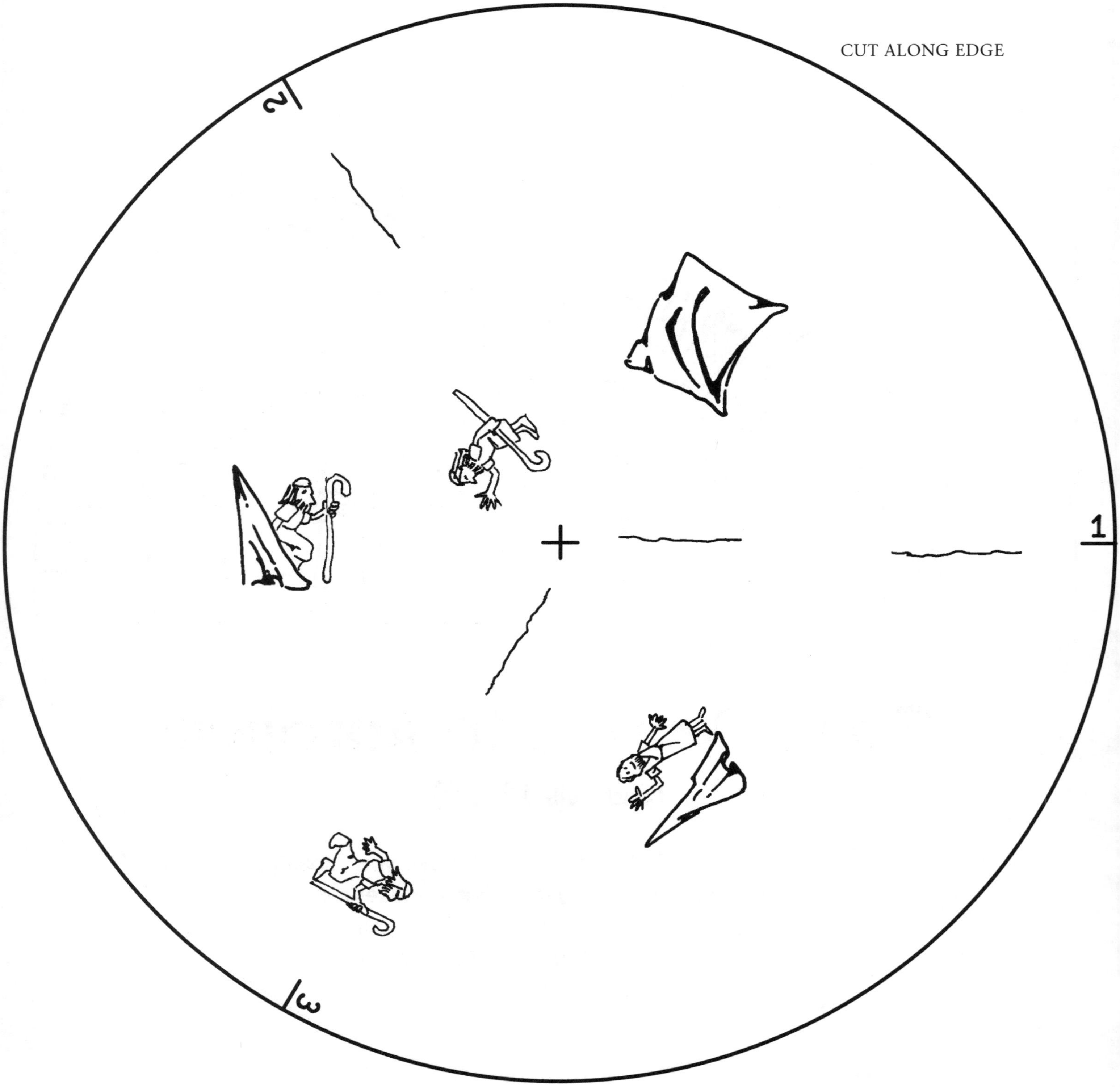

CUT ALONG EDGE
1
2
3

Baby Isaac (Genesis 21:1-8)

Sarah became pregnant and bore a son to Abraham in his old age, at the very time God had promised him. Abraham gave the name Isaac to the son Sarah bore him (Genesis 21:2-4).

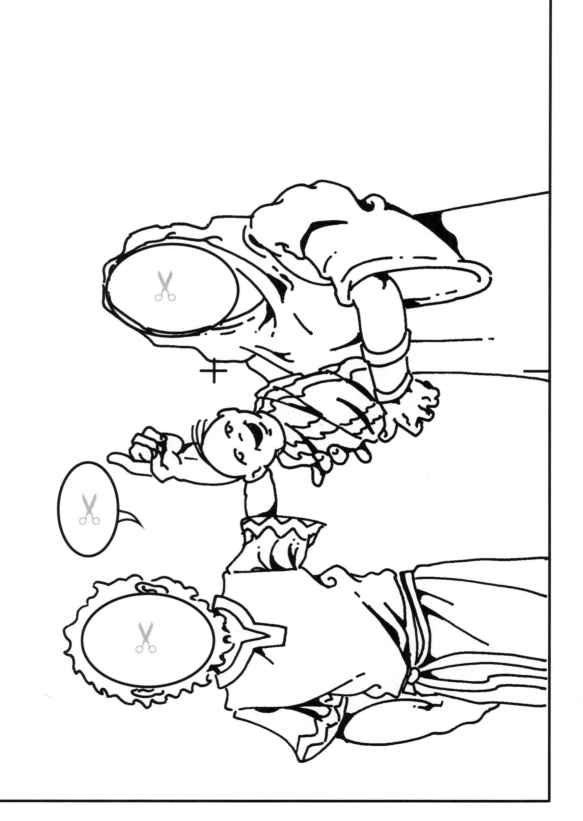

CUT ALONG EDGE

Baby Isaac

Bottom

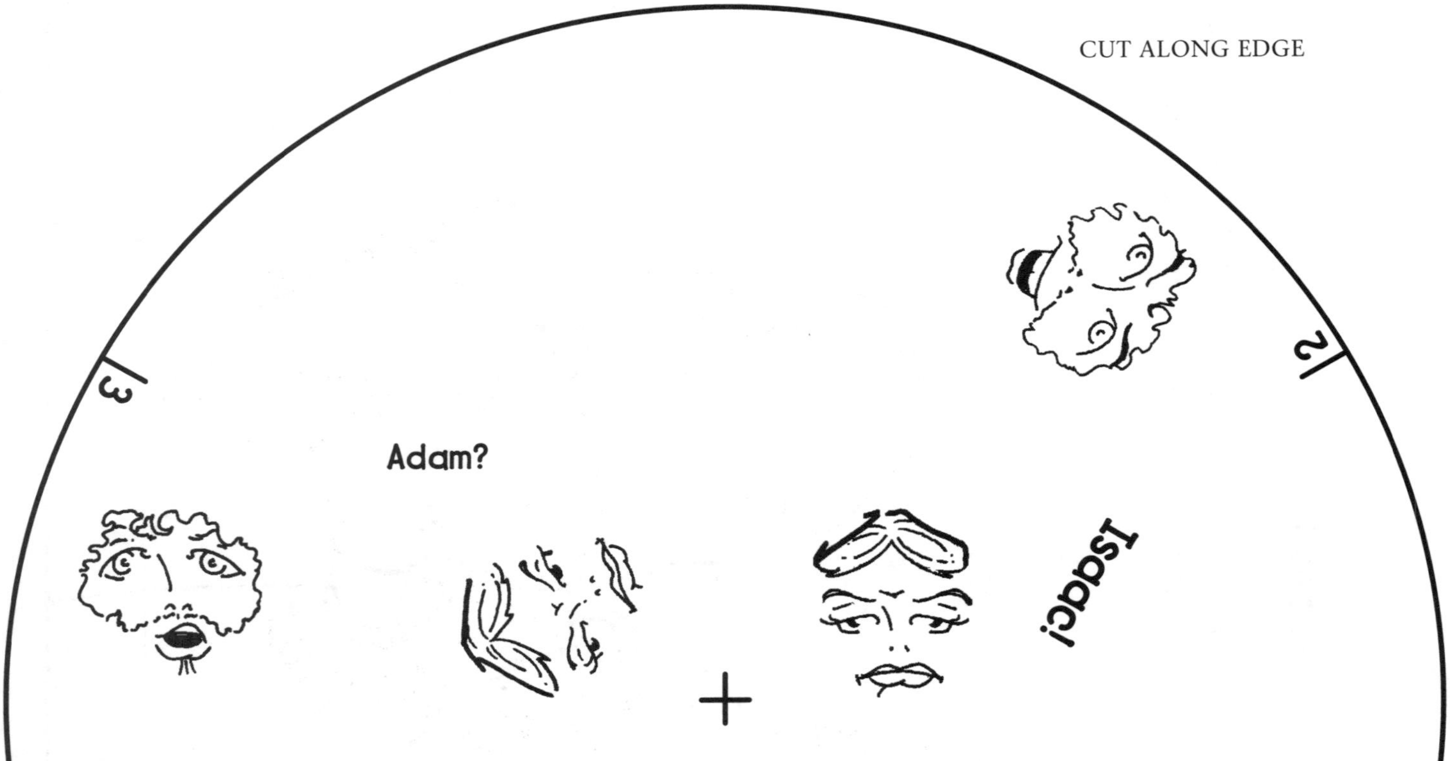

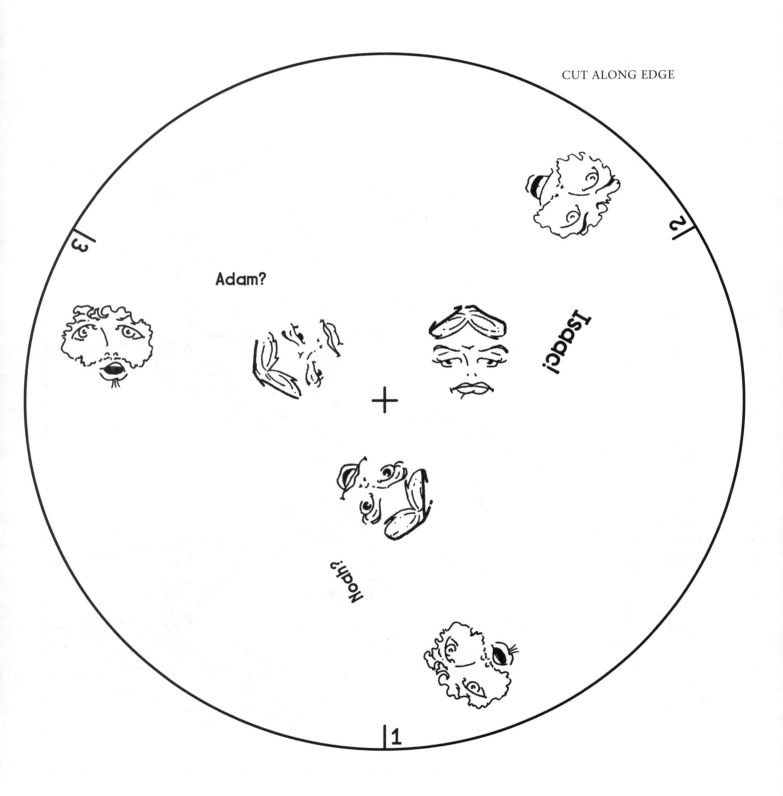

CUT ALONG EDGE
Adam?
Isaac!
Noah?
1
2
3

Top

Jacob's
Dream
(Genesis 28:10-22)

CUT ALONG EDGE

Jacob's Dream

Bottom

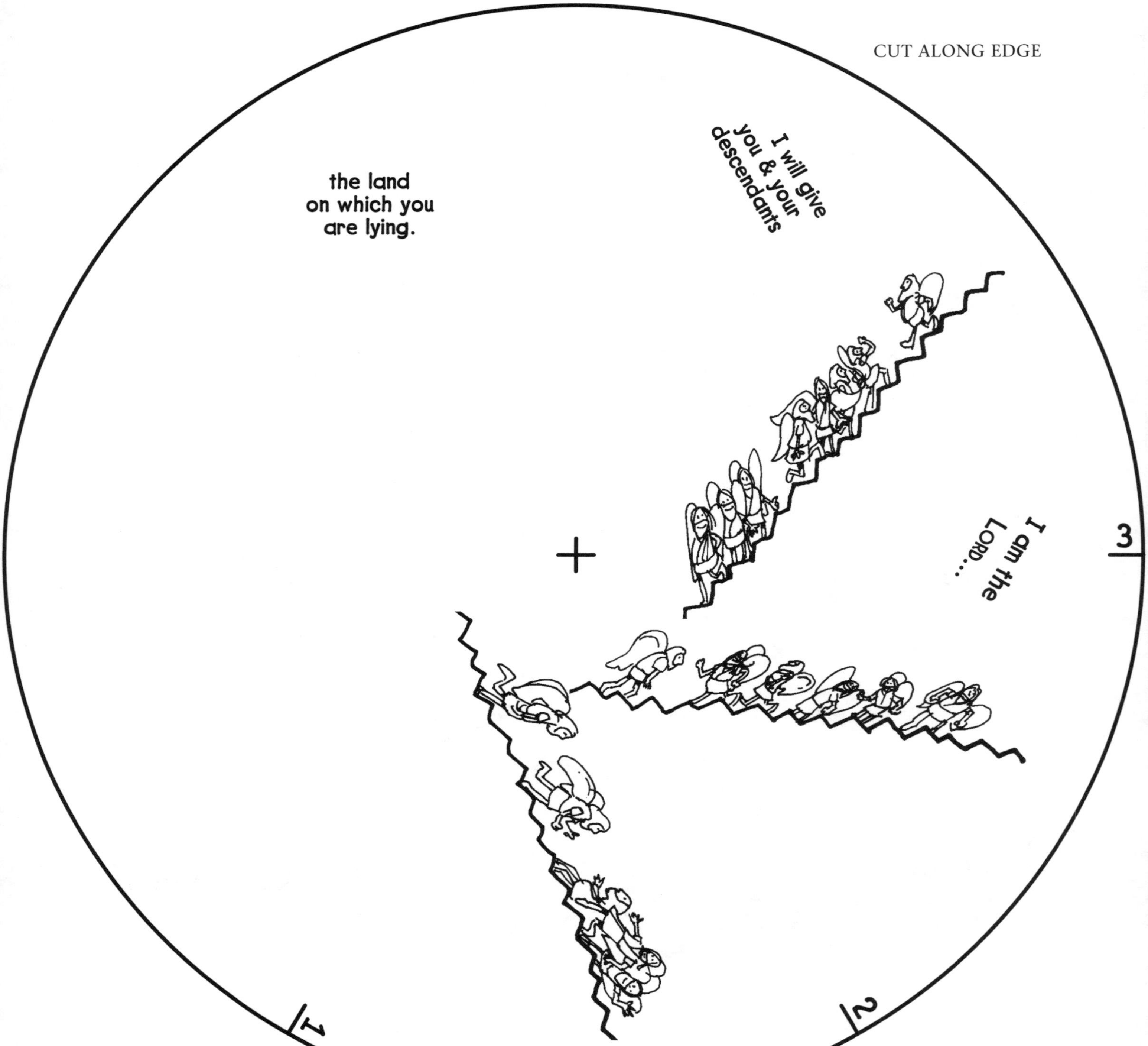
CUT ALONG EDGE
I will give
you & your
descendants
the land
on which you
are lying.
I am the
LORD...
1
2
3

Joseph's Colorful Coat

(Genesis 37:1-36)

CUT ALONG EDGE

Joseph's Colorful Coat

Bottom

CUT ALONG EDGE
3
Joseph, a young man of seventeen, tended the flocks with his brothers.
Jacob loved Joseph more than any of his other sons. He gave Joseph a coat of many colors.
2
Joseph's brothers were jealous & sold him to merchants who took him to Egypt.
1

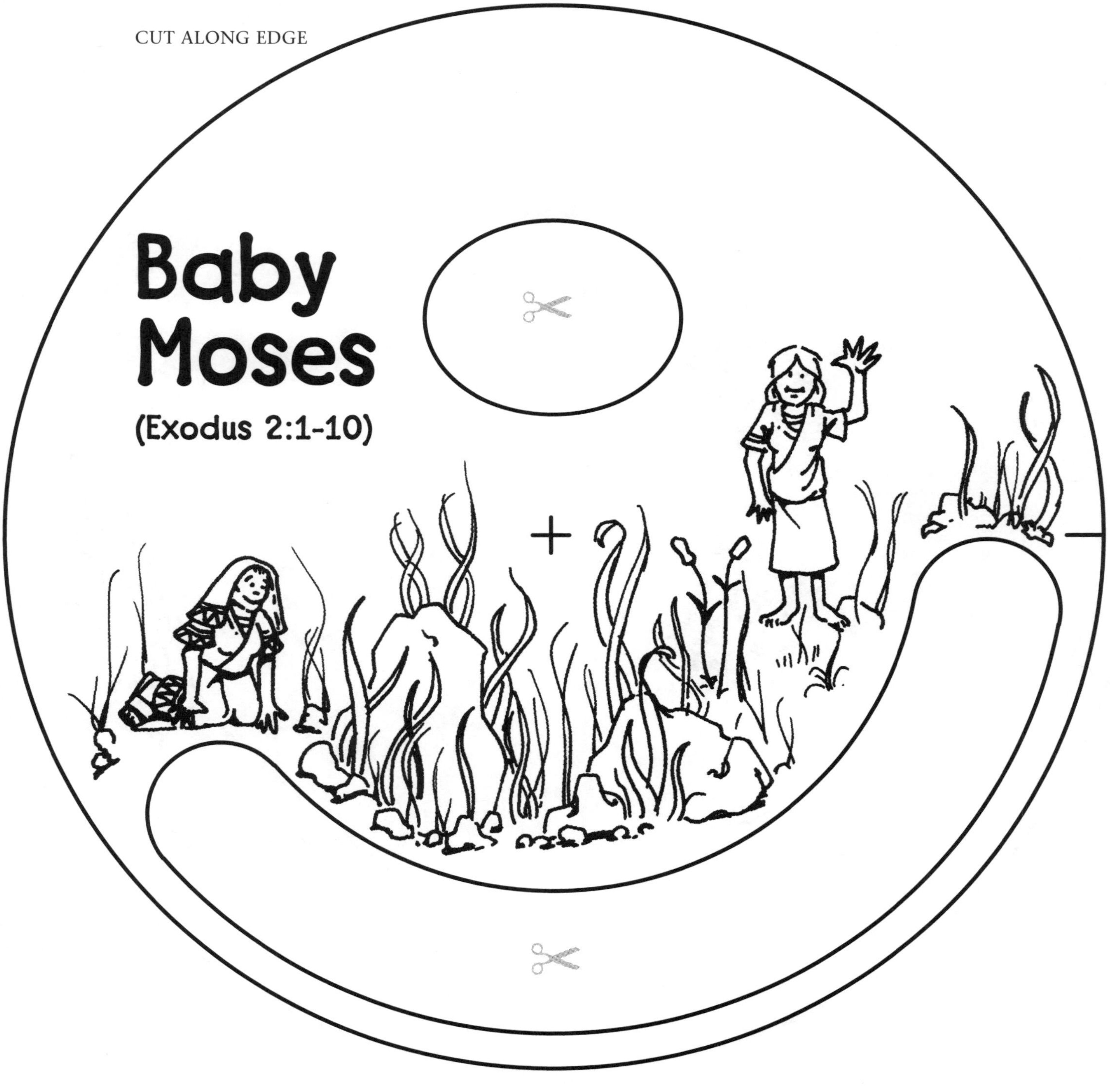
CUT ALONG EDGE
Baby Moses
(Exodus 2:1-10)

Baby Moses

Bottom

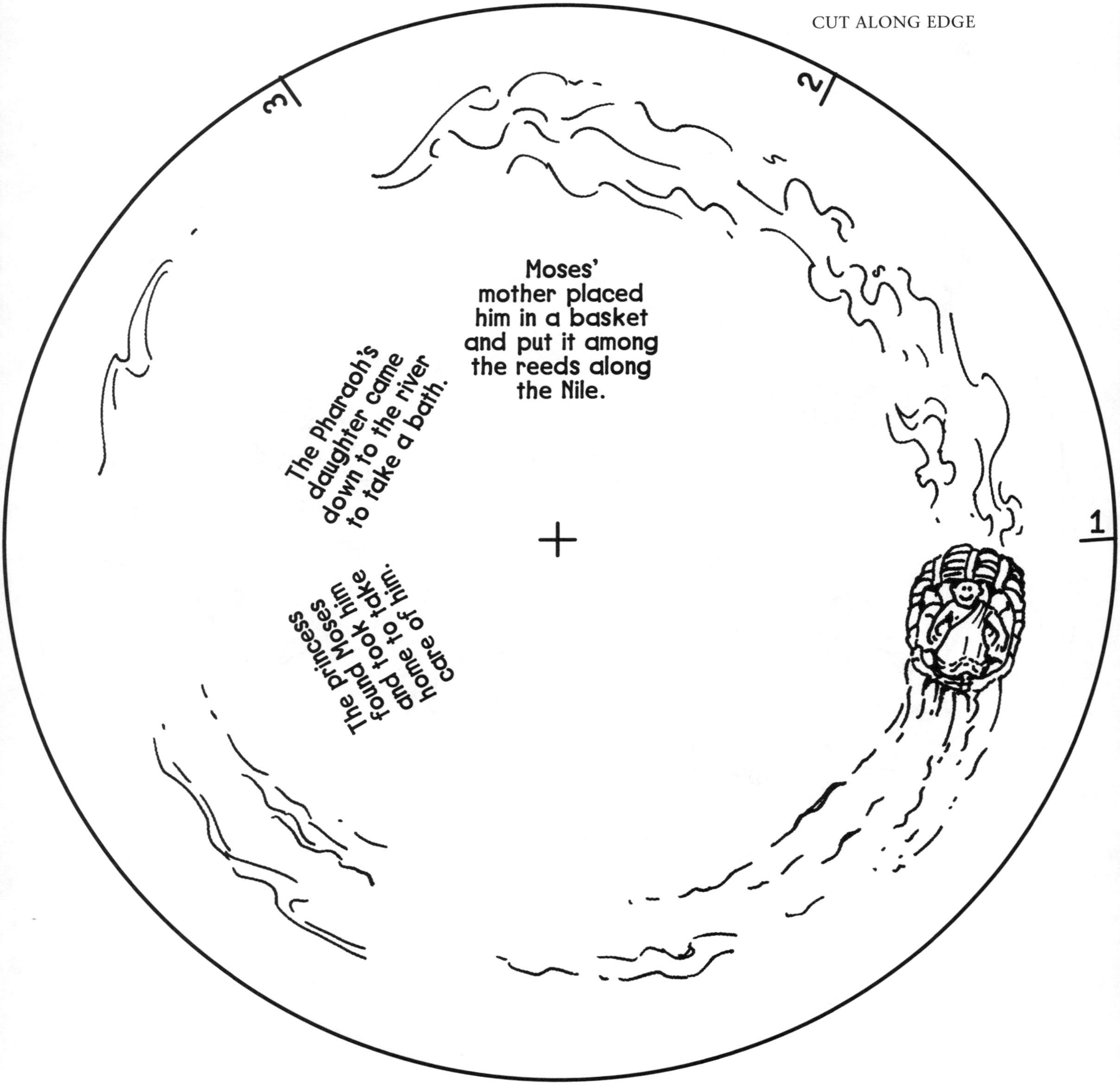
CUT ALONG EDGE
1
2
3
Moses' mother placed him in a basket and put it among the reeds along the Nile.
The Pharaoh's daughter came down to the river to take a bath.
The princess found Moses and took him home to take care of him.

Crossing the Red Sea

(Exodus 3:1-14:31)

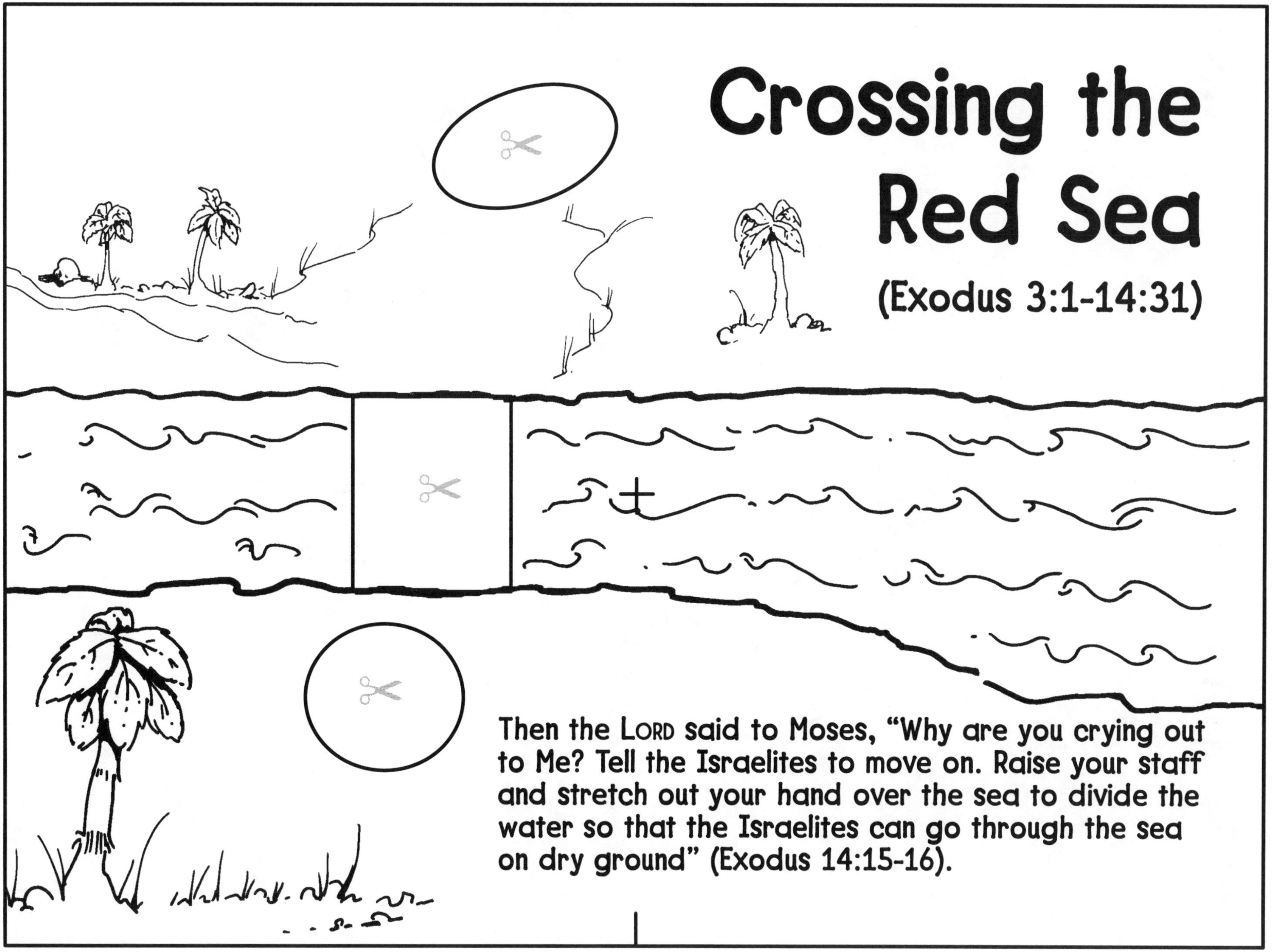

Then the LORD said to Moses, "Why are you crying out to Me? Tell the Israelites to move on. Raise your staff and stretch out your hand over the sea to divide the water so that the Israelites can go through the sea on dry ground" (Exodus 14:15-16).

CUT ALONG EDGE

Crossing the Red Sea

Bottom

CUT ALONG EDGE

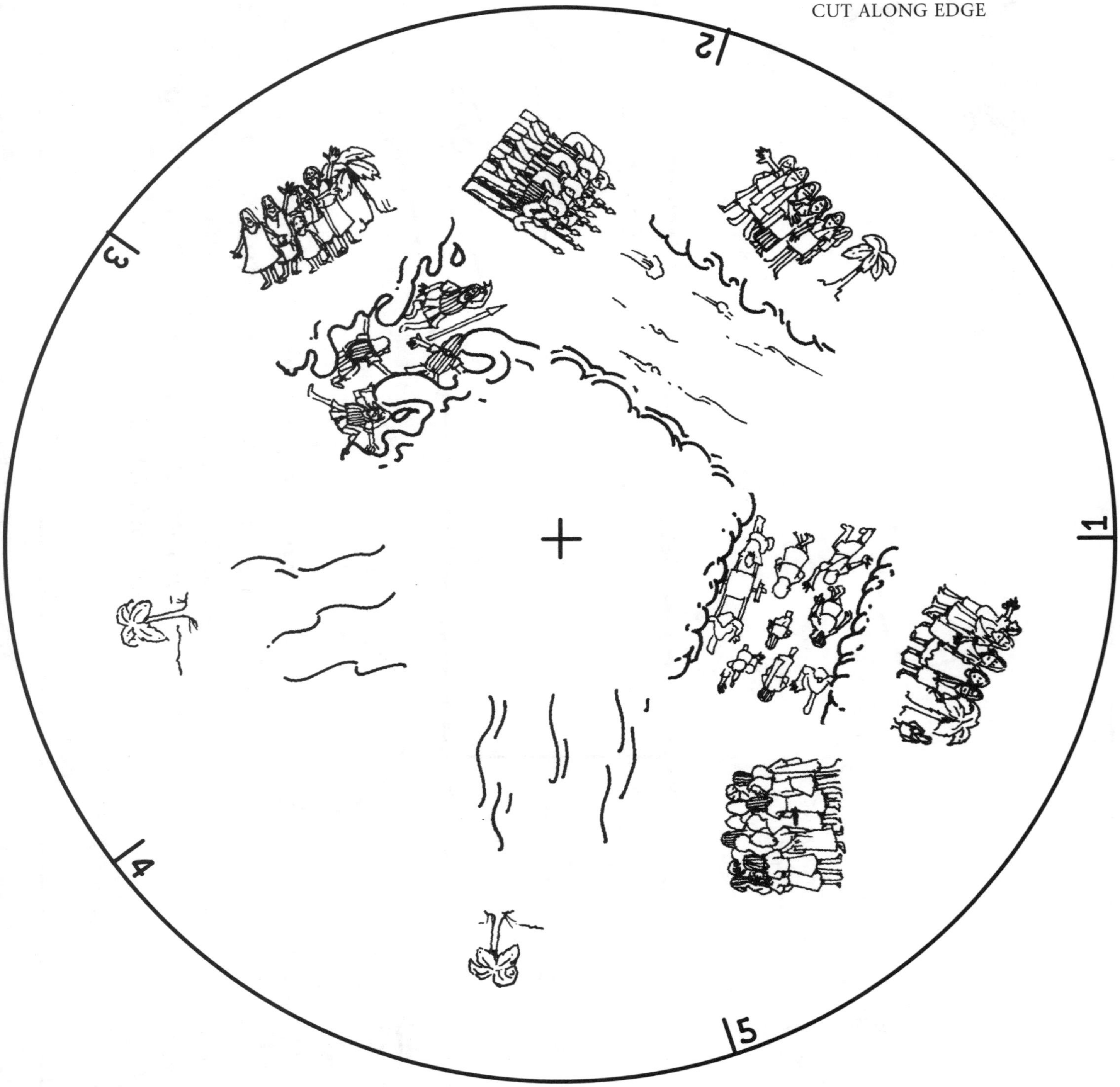

1
2
3
4
5

Top

The Walls of Jericho

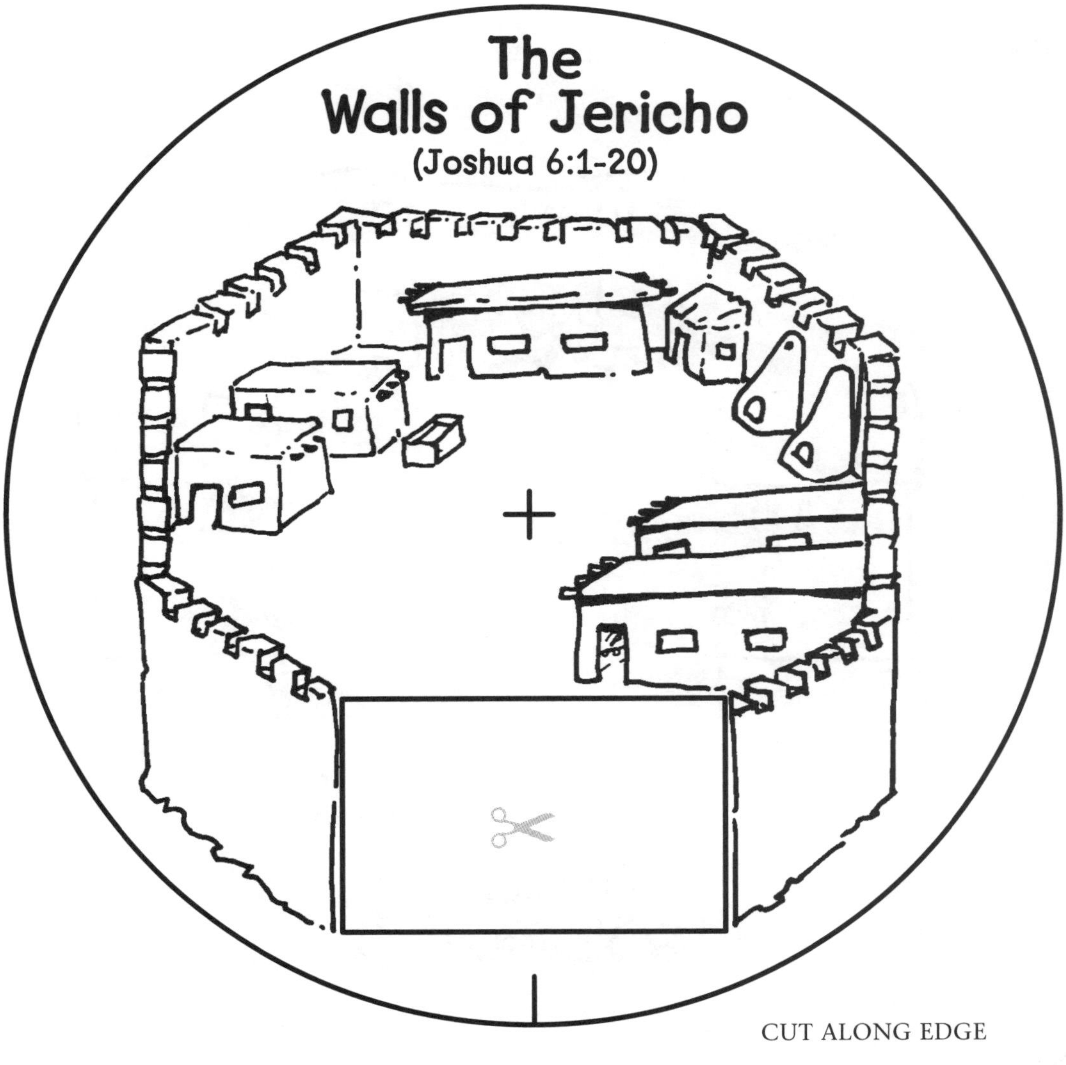
The
Walls of Jericho
(Joshua 6:1-20)

CUT ALONG EDGE

The Walls of Jericho

Bottom

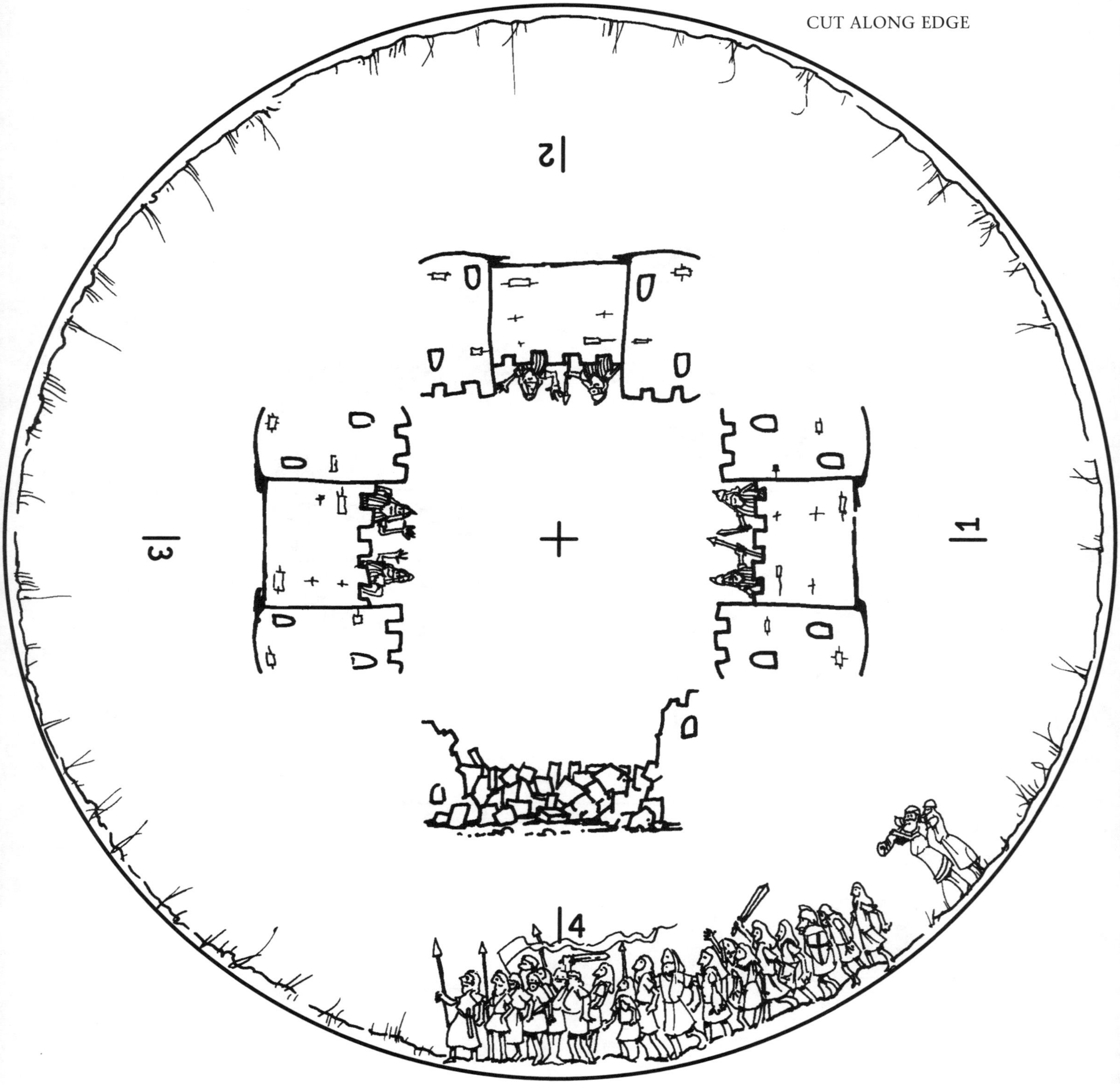

CUT ALONG EDGE
2
3
1
4

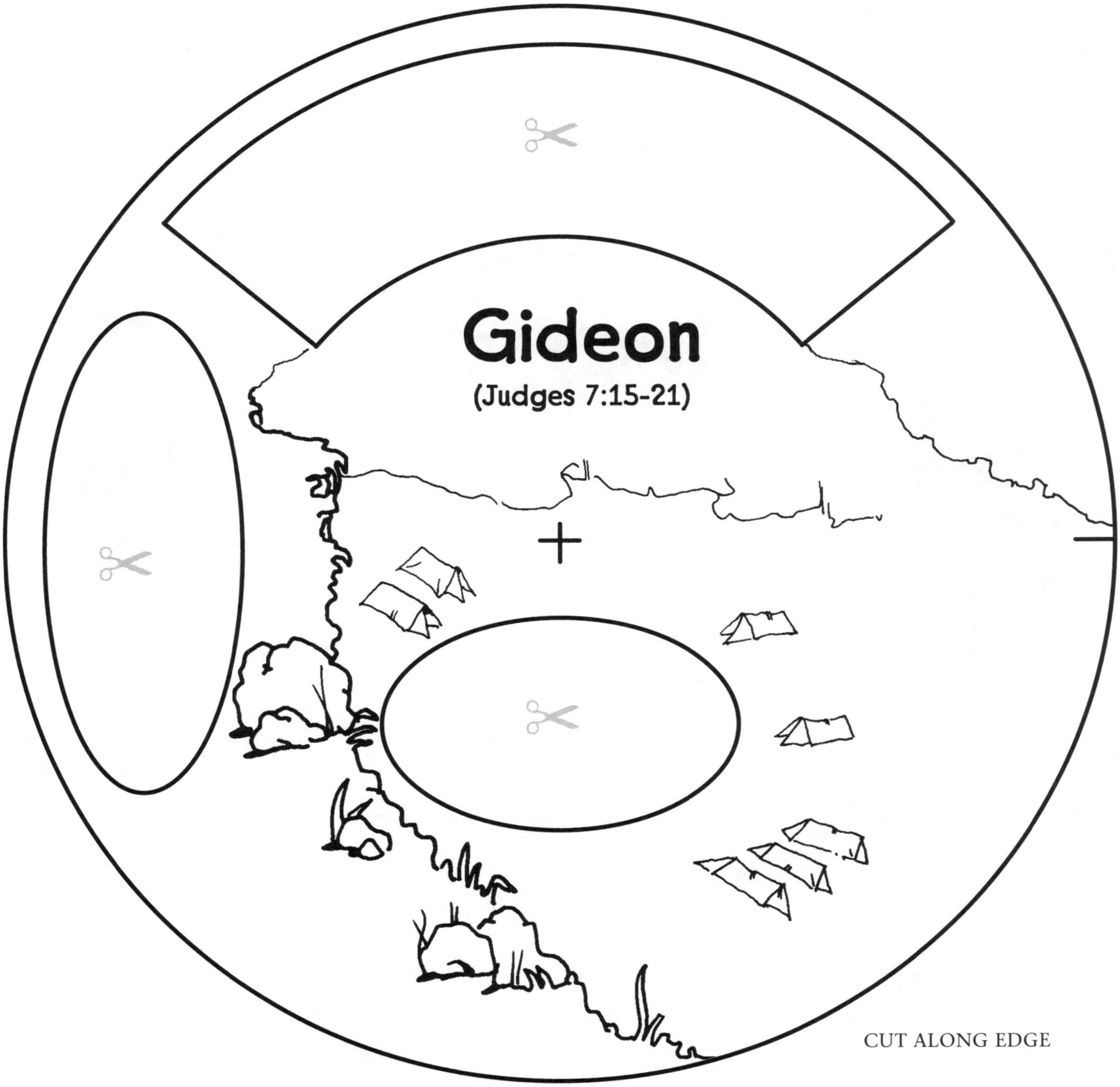
Gideon
(Judges 7:15-21)
CUT ALONG EDGE

Gideon

Bottom

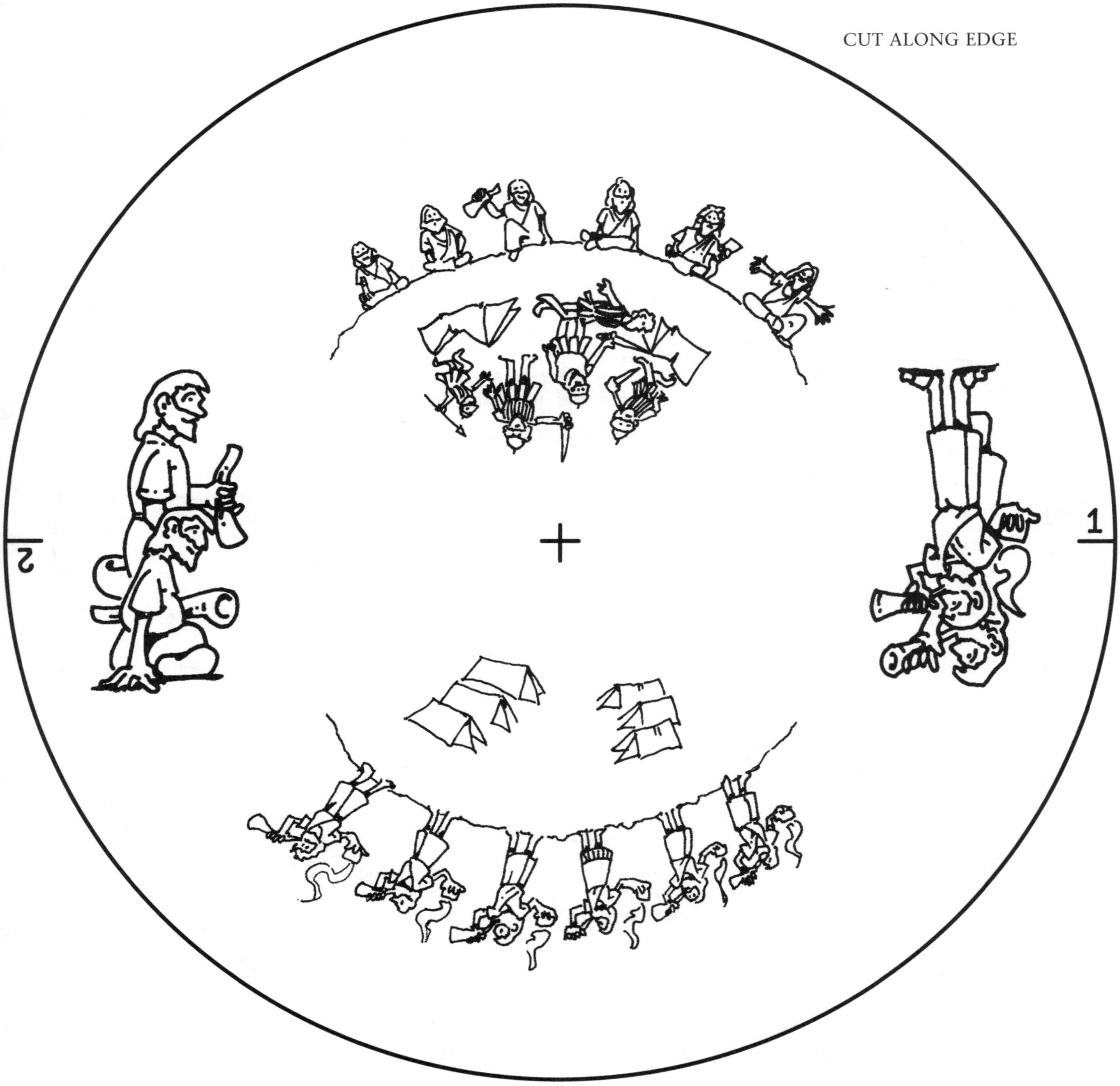
CUT ALONG EDGE
1
2

Samson

(Judges 16:4-30)

CUT ALONG EDGE

Samson

Bottom

CUT ALONG EDGE

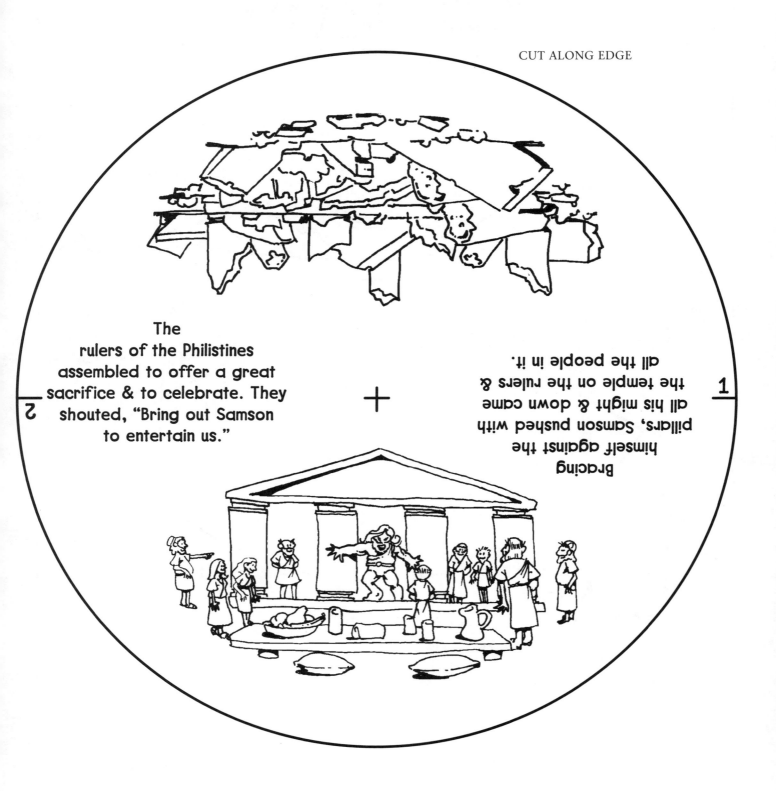

The rulers of the Philistines assembled to offer a great sacrifice & to celebrate. They shouted, "Bring out Samson to entertain us."

2

1

Bracing himself against the pillars, Samson pushed with all his might & down came the temple on the rulers & all the people in it.

David & Goliath

David &
Goliath
(1 Samuel 17:1-50)

CUT ALONG EDGE

David & Goliath

Bottom

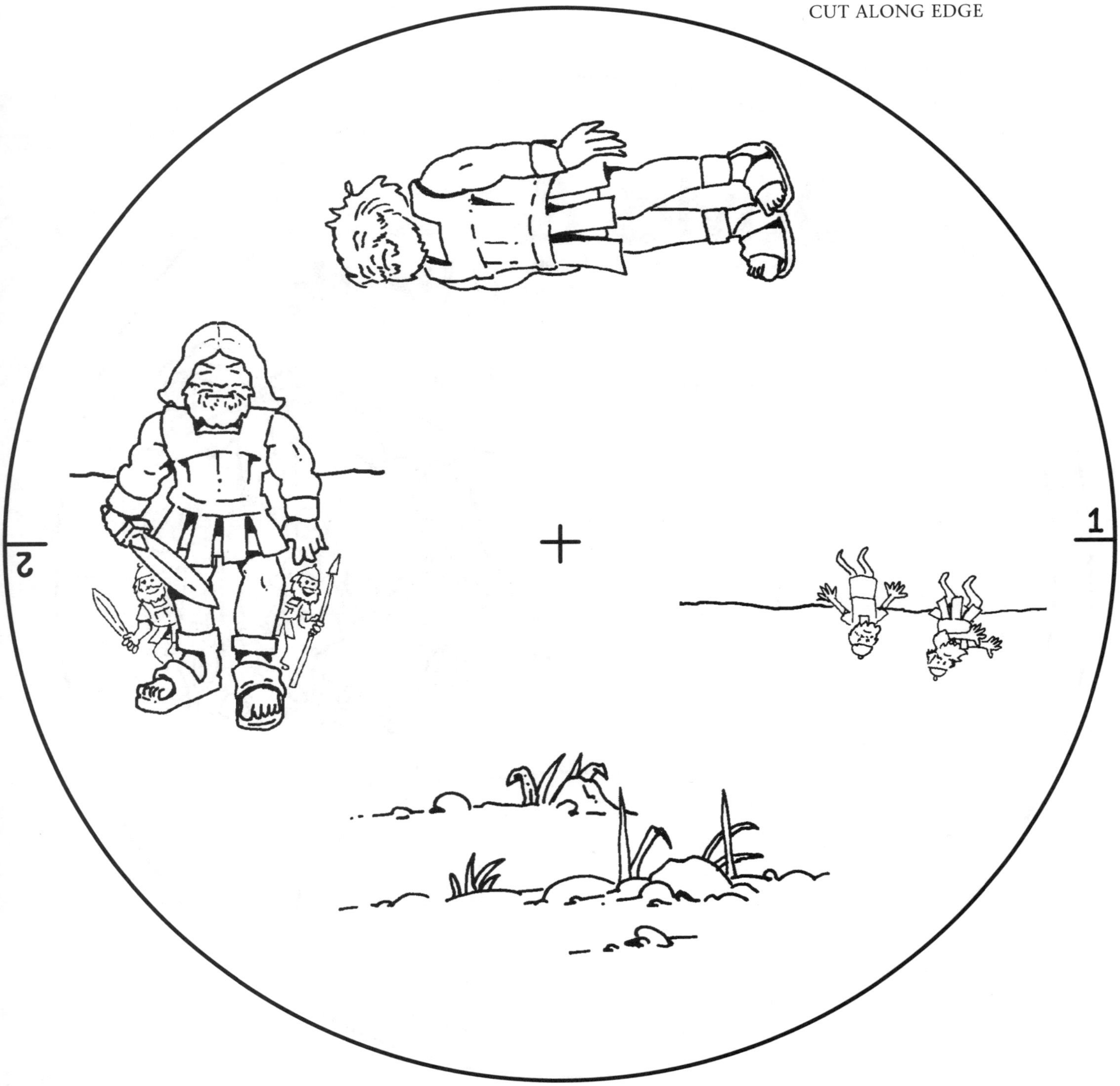

CUT ALONG EDGE
1
2

Top

Daniel & the Lions

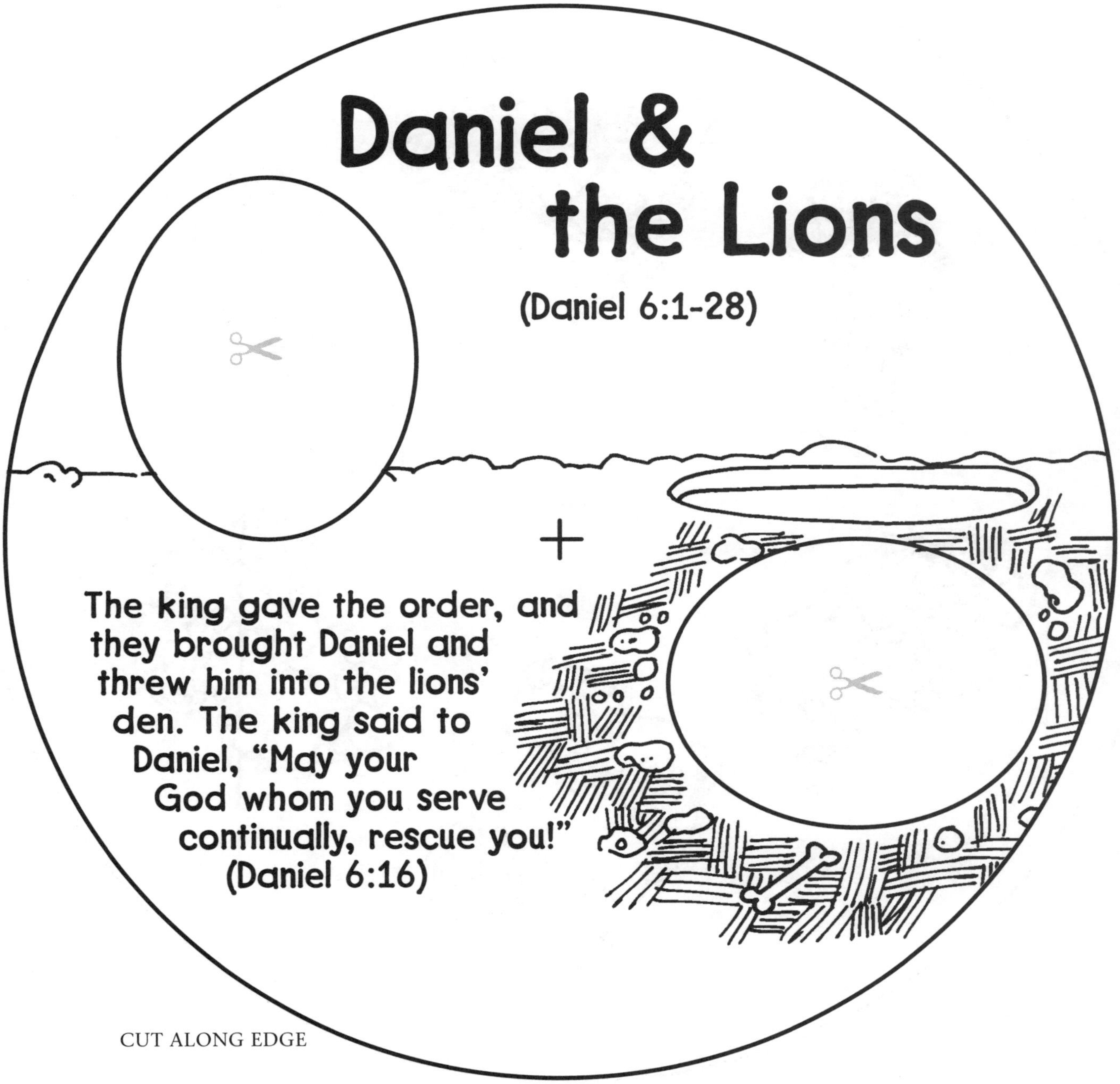
Daniel & the Lions
(Daniel 6:1-28)
The king gave the order, and they brought Daniel and threw him into the lions' den. The king said to Daniel, "May your God whom you serve continually, rescue you!"
(Daniel 6:16)
CUT ALONG EDGE

Daniel & the Lions

Bottom

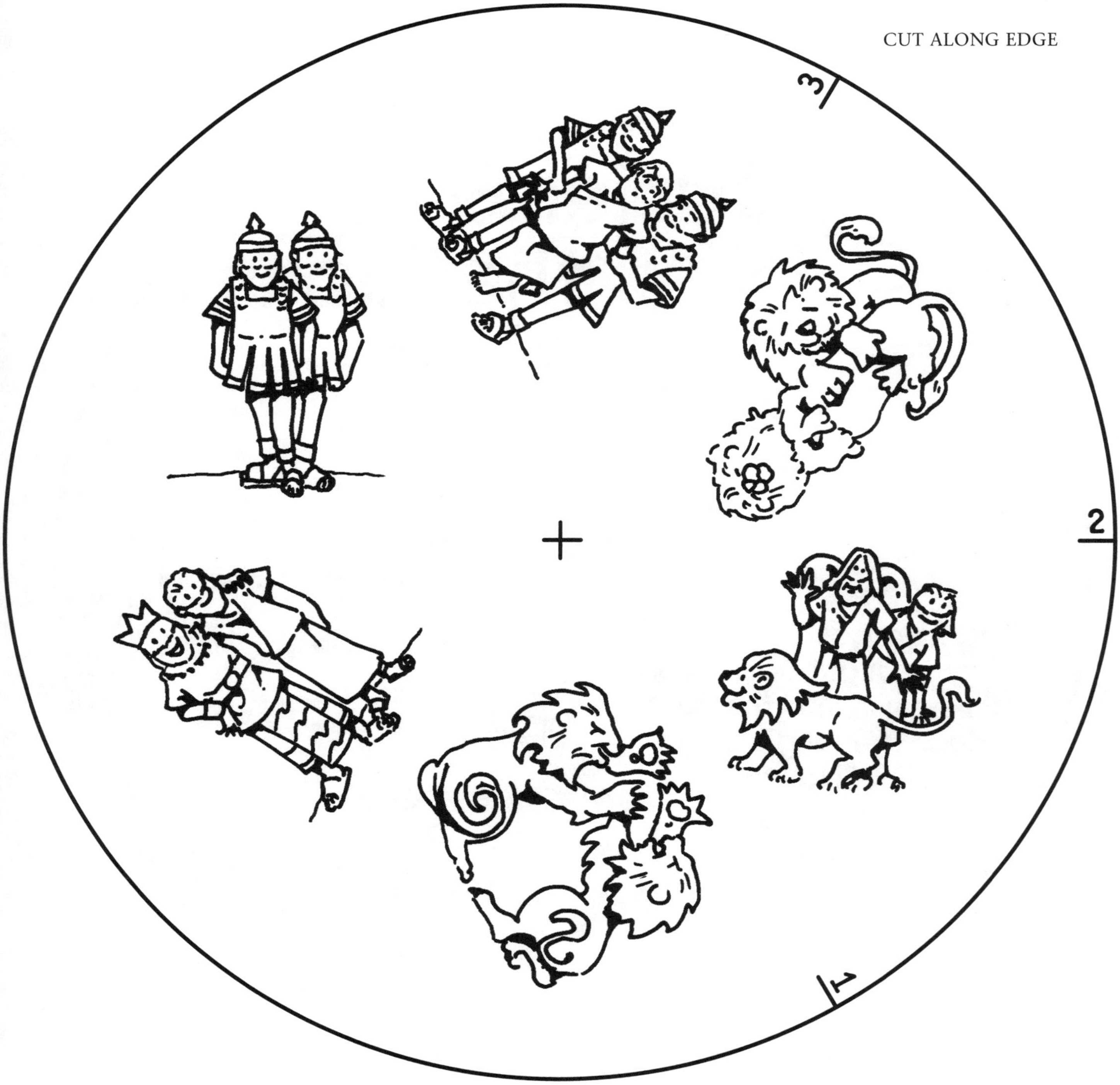
CUT ALONG EDGE
3
2
1

Jonah & the Big Fish

Jonah & the Big Fish

(The Book of Jonah)

"Pick me up and throw me
into the sea," [Jonah said],
"and it will become calm.
I know that it is my fault
that this great storm
has come upon you."
(Jonah 1:12)

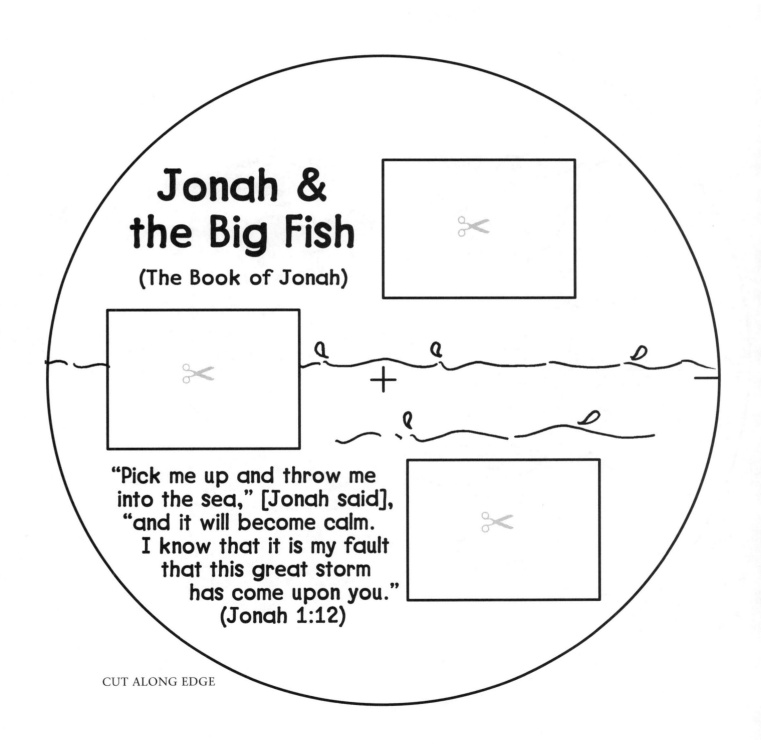

CUT ALONG EDGE

Jonah & the Big Fish

Bottom

CUT ALONG EDGE

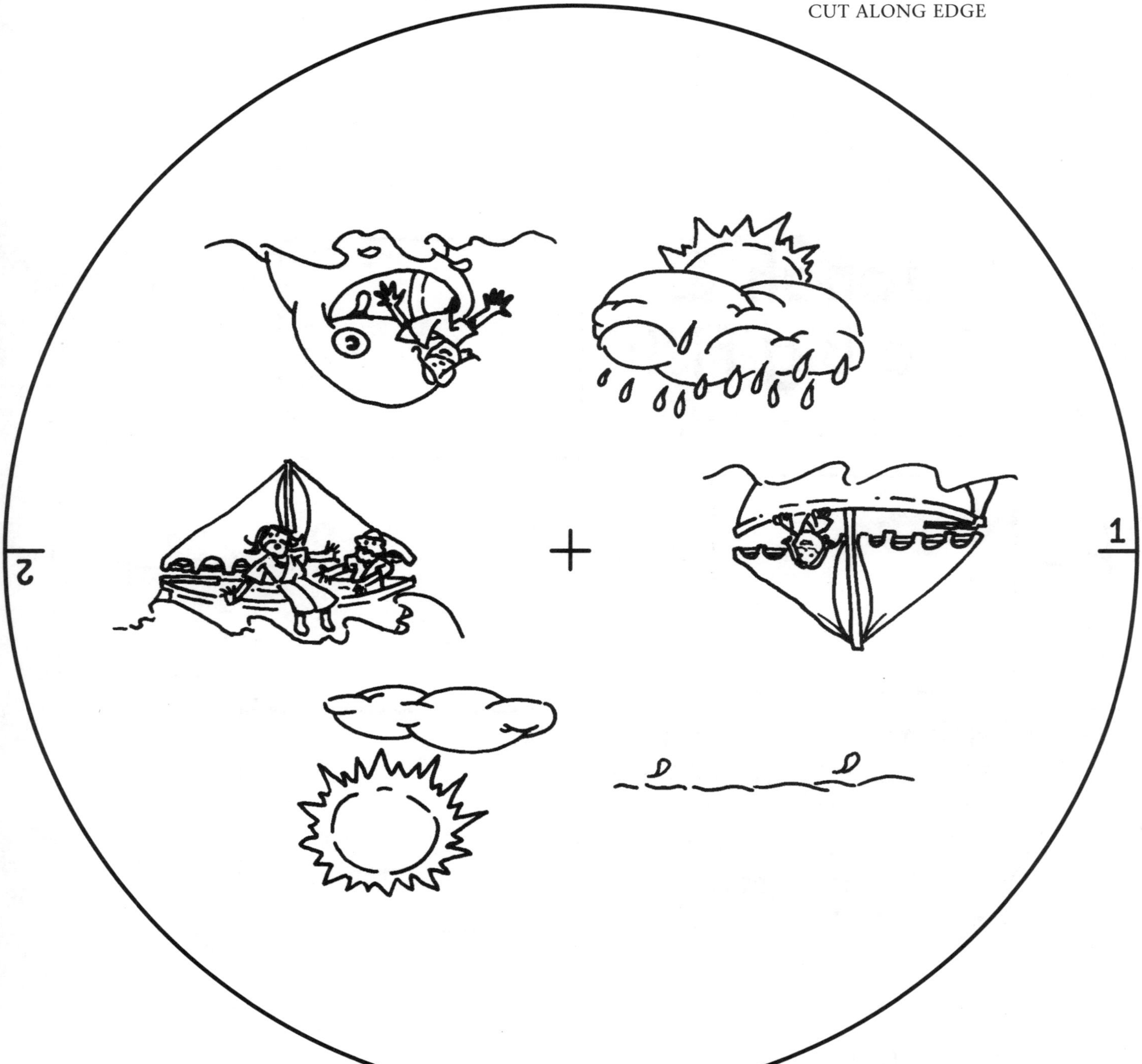
1
2

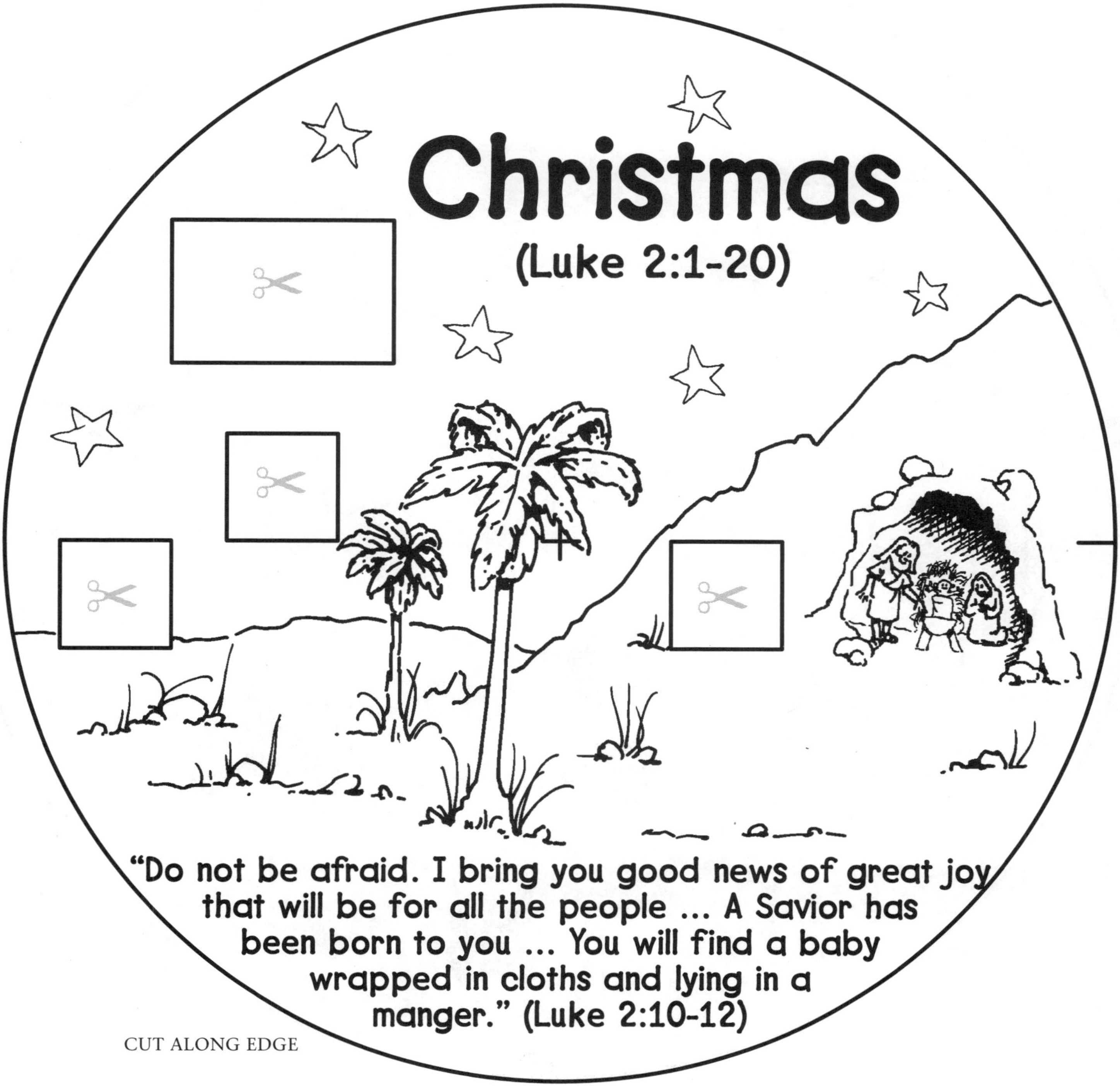
Christmas
(Luke 2:1-20)
"Do not be afraid. I bring you good news of great joy that will be for all the people ... A Savior has been born to you ... You will find a baby wrapped in cloths and lying in a manger." (Luke 2:10-12)

CUT ALONG EDGE

Christmas

Bottom

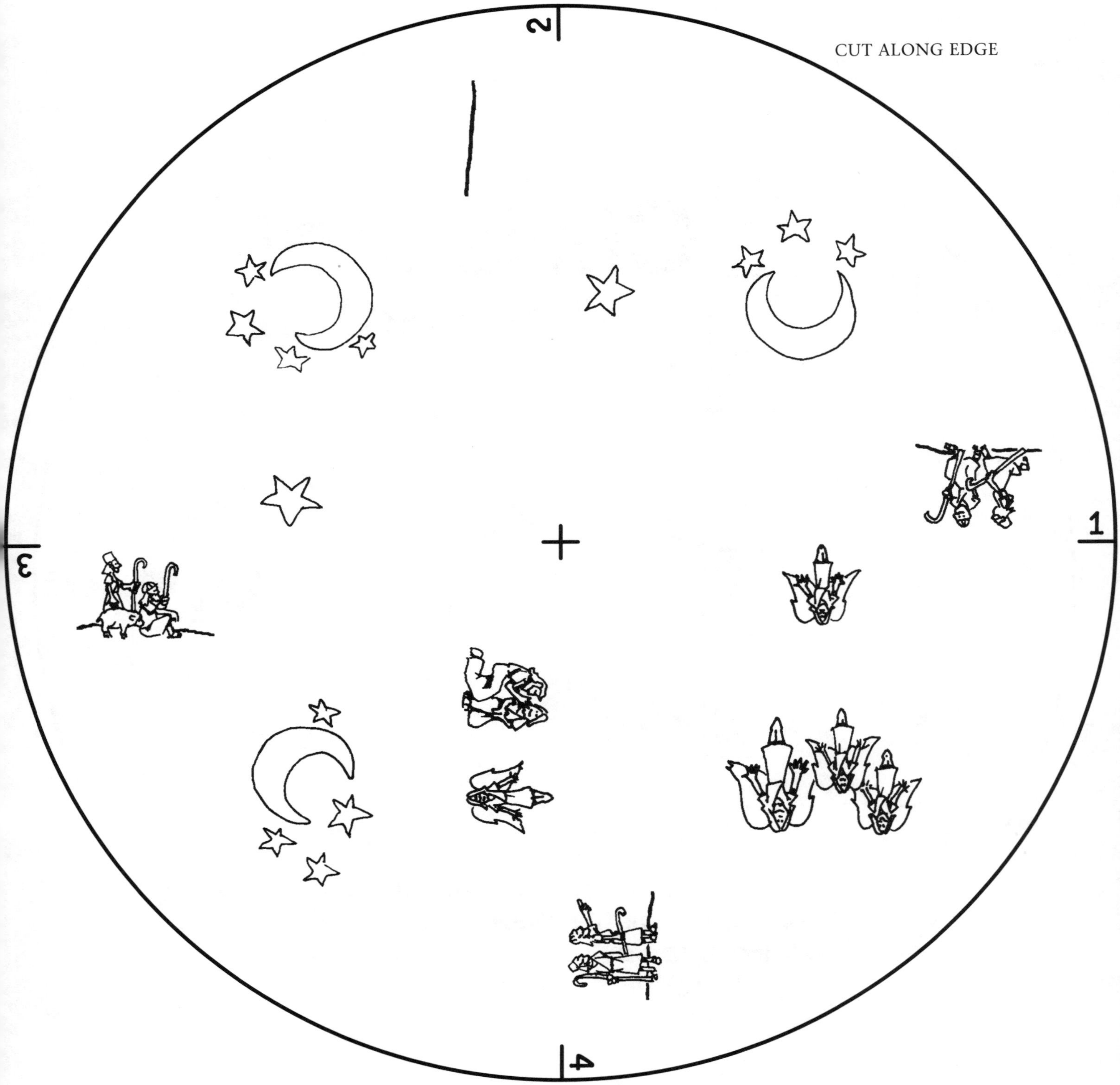
CUT ALONG EDGE
1
2
3
4

Top

The Wise Men Visit Jesus

The Wise Men
Visit Jesus
(Matthew 2:1-12)

CUT ALONG EDGE

The Wise Men Visit Jesus

Bottom

CUT ALONG EDGE

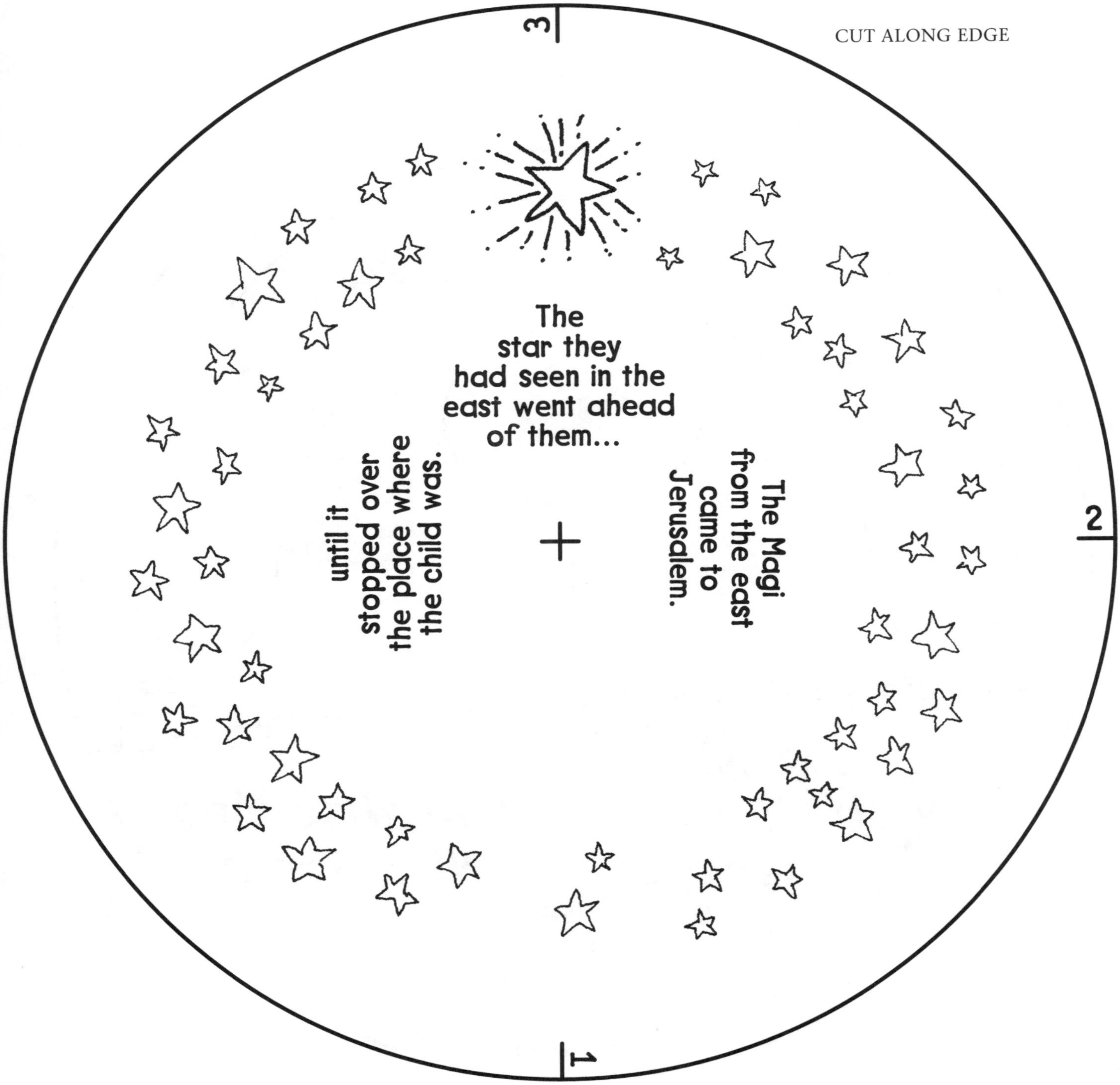
3
The star they had seen in the east went ahead of them...
The Magi from the east came to Jerusalem.
2
until it stopped over the place where the child was.
1

Top

Young Jesus in the Temple

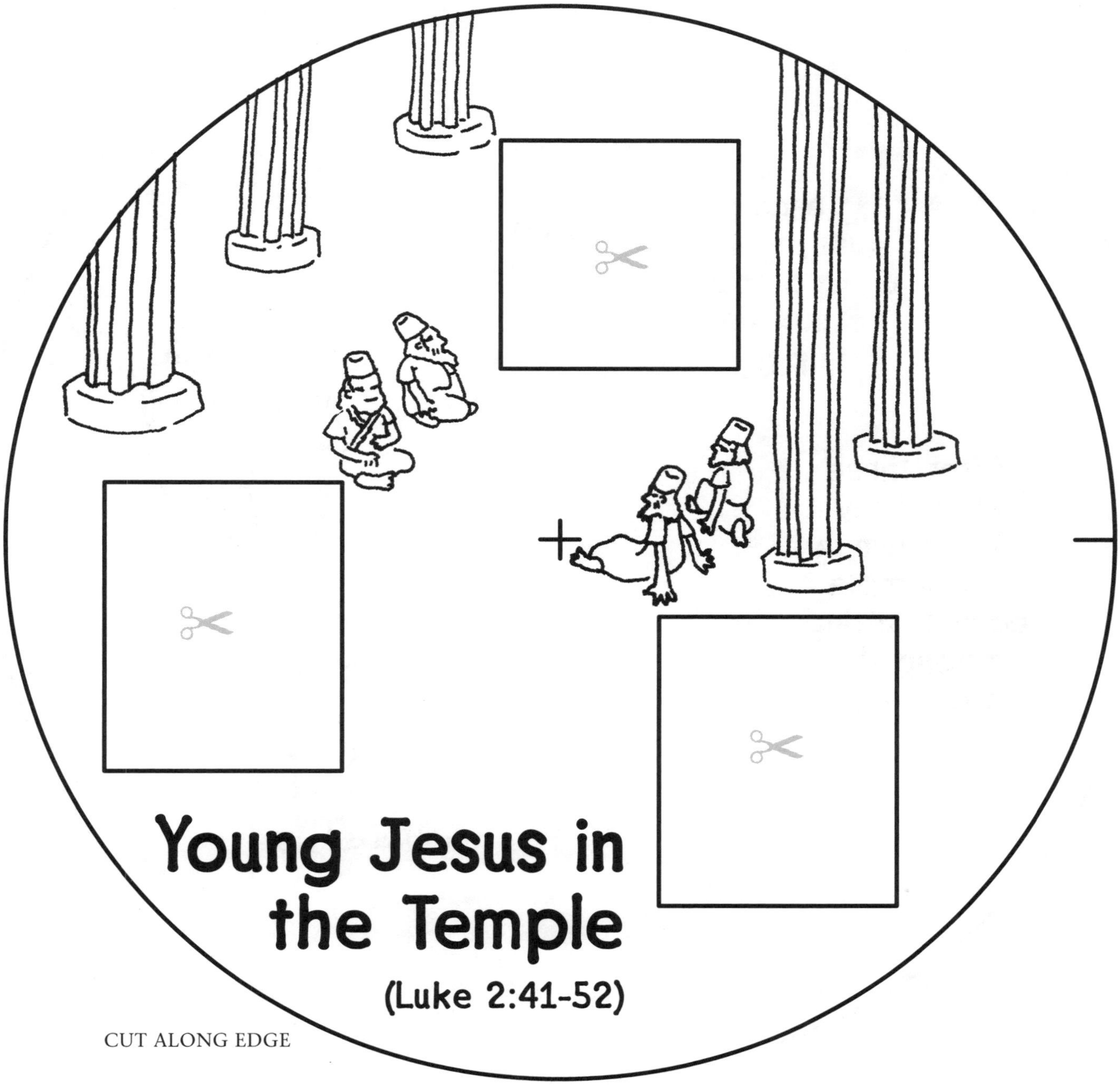
Young Jesus in the Temple
(Luke 2:41-52)
CUT ALONG EDGE

Young Jesus in the Temple

Bottom

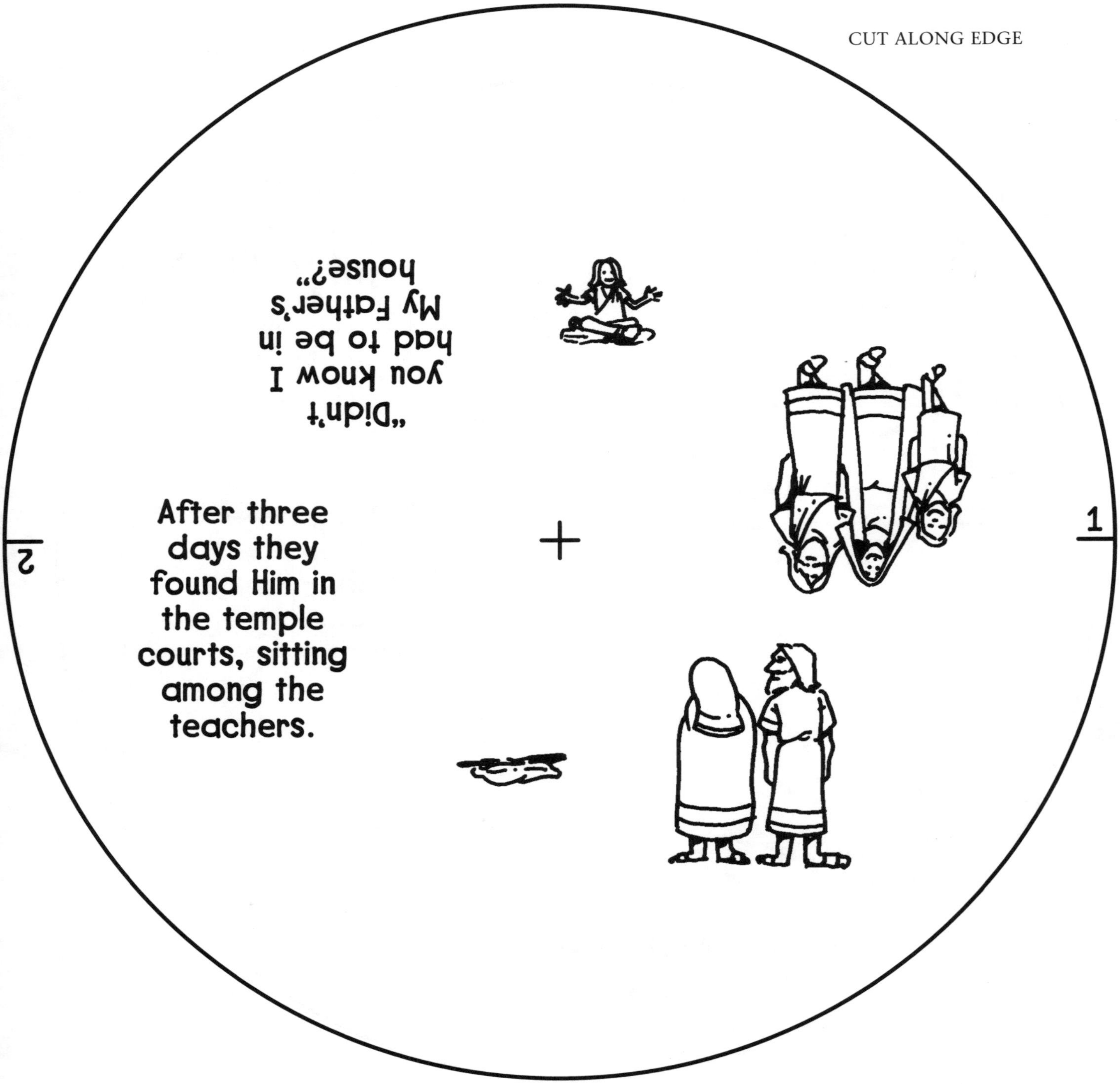
CUT ALONG EDGE
1
2
After three days they found Him in the temple courts, sitting among the teachers.
"Didn't you know I had to be in My Father's house?"

Jesus' Baptism

Jesus' Baptism
(Matthew 3:13-17)
CUT ALONG EDGE

Jesus' Baptism

Bottom

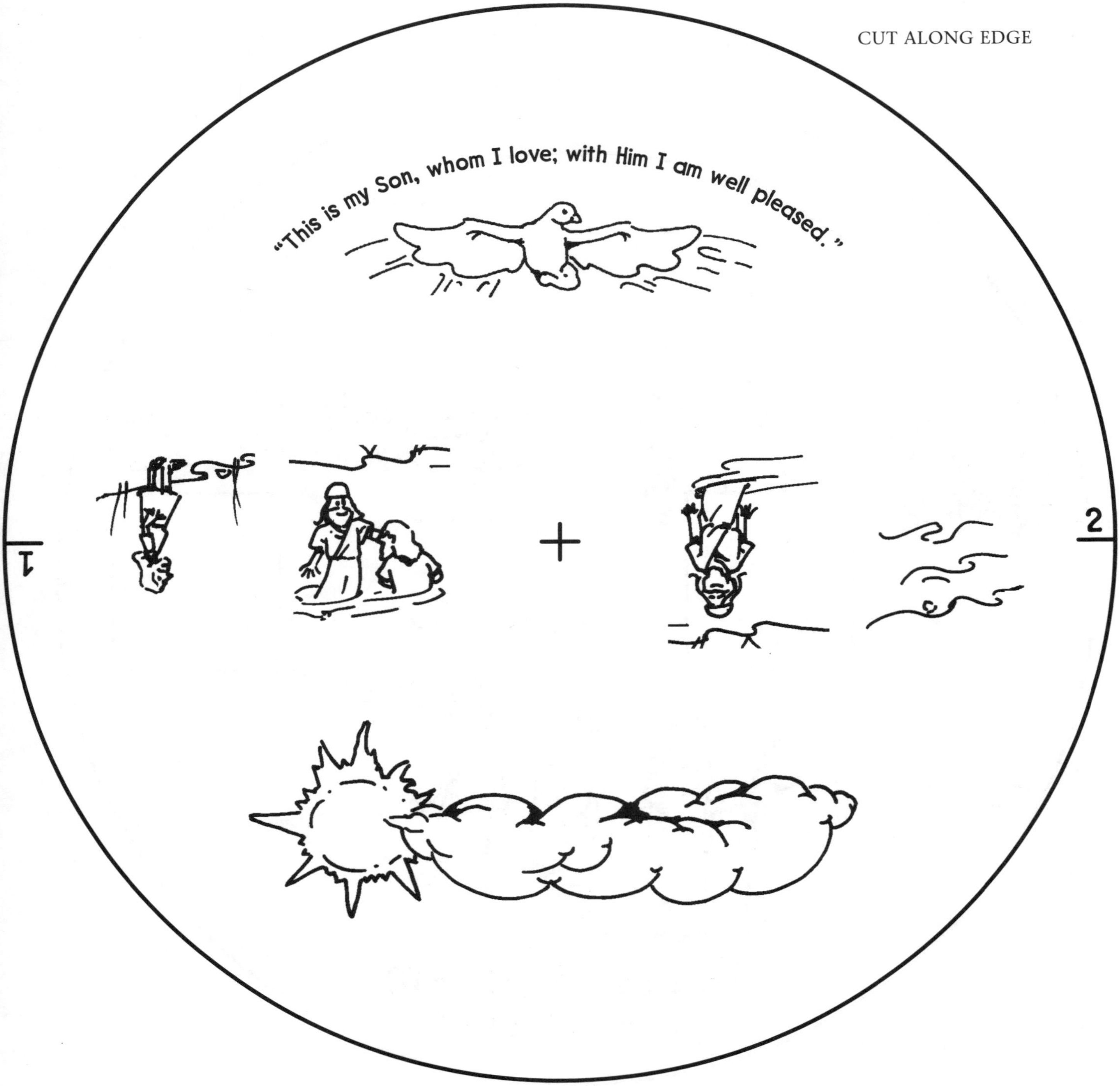
CUT ALONG EDGE
"This is my Son, whom I love; with Him I am well pleased."
2

Top

Jesus Stills the Storm

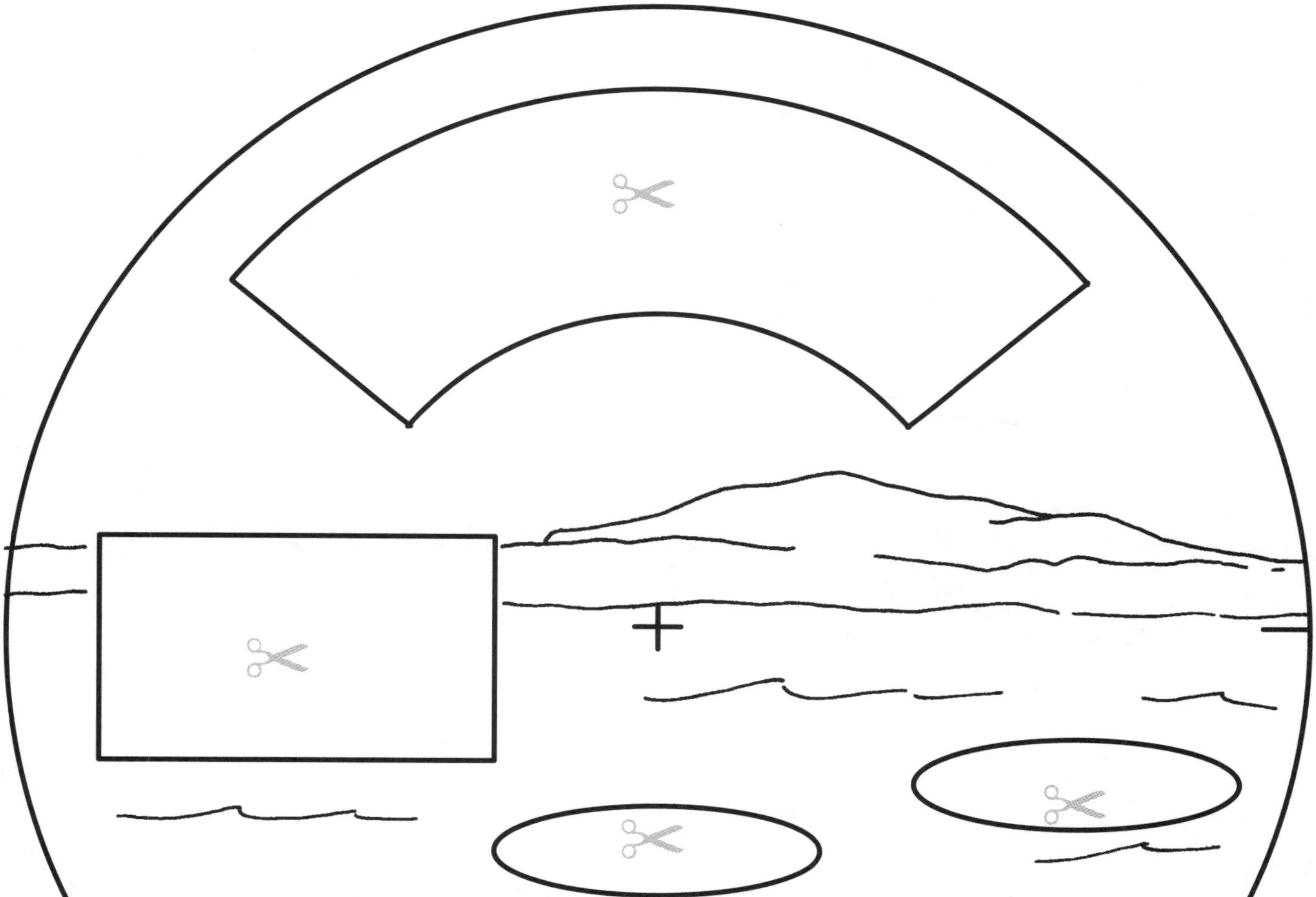

Jesus Stills the Storm
(Matthew 8:23-27)

"You of little faith, why are you so afraid?"
Then He got up and rebuked the winds
and the waves, and it was
completely calm.
(Matthew 8:26)

CUT ALONG EDGE

Jesus Stills the Storm

Bottom

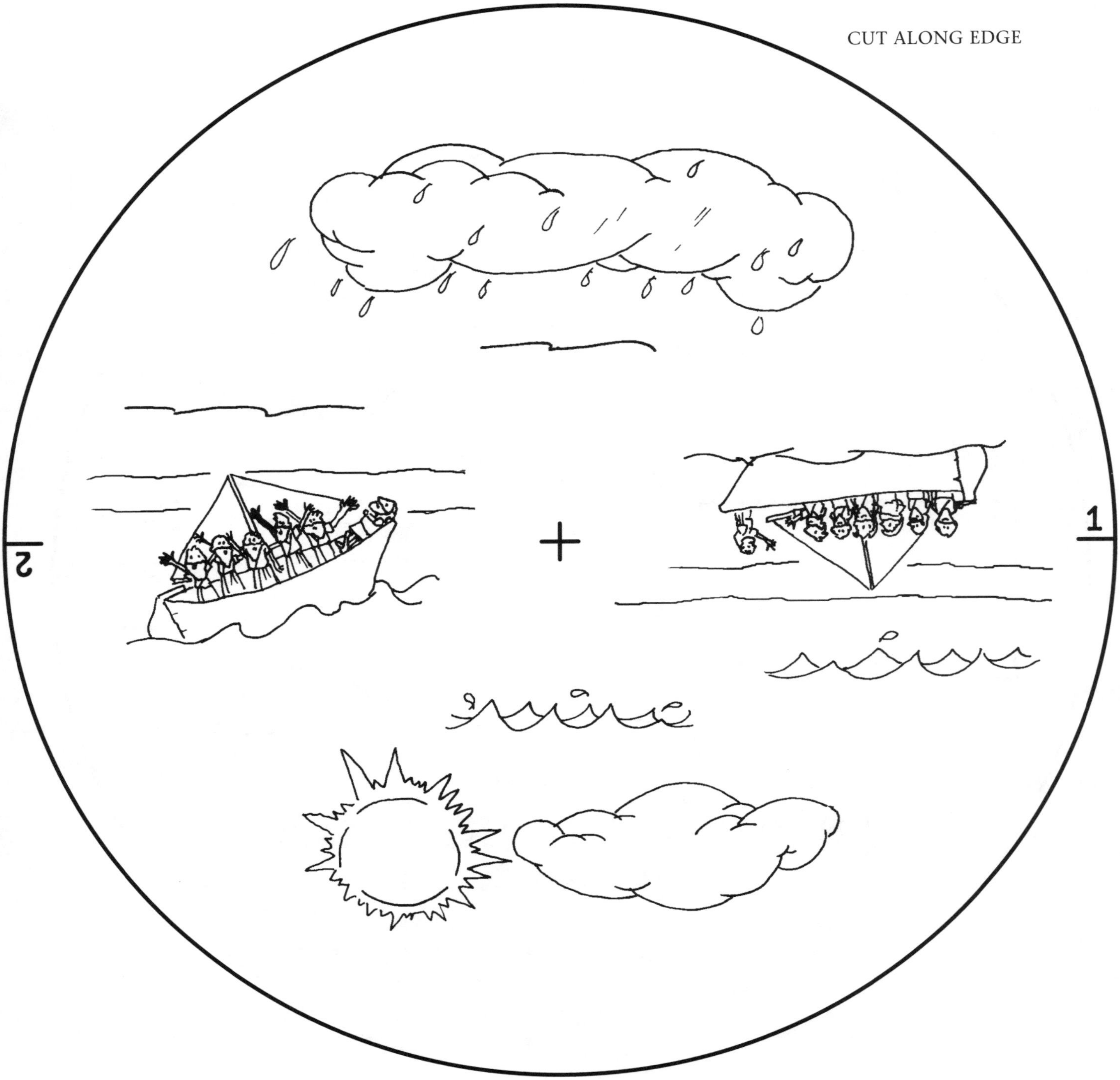
CUT ALONG EDGE
1
2

Top

Jesus Raises Jairus' Daughter

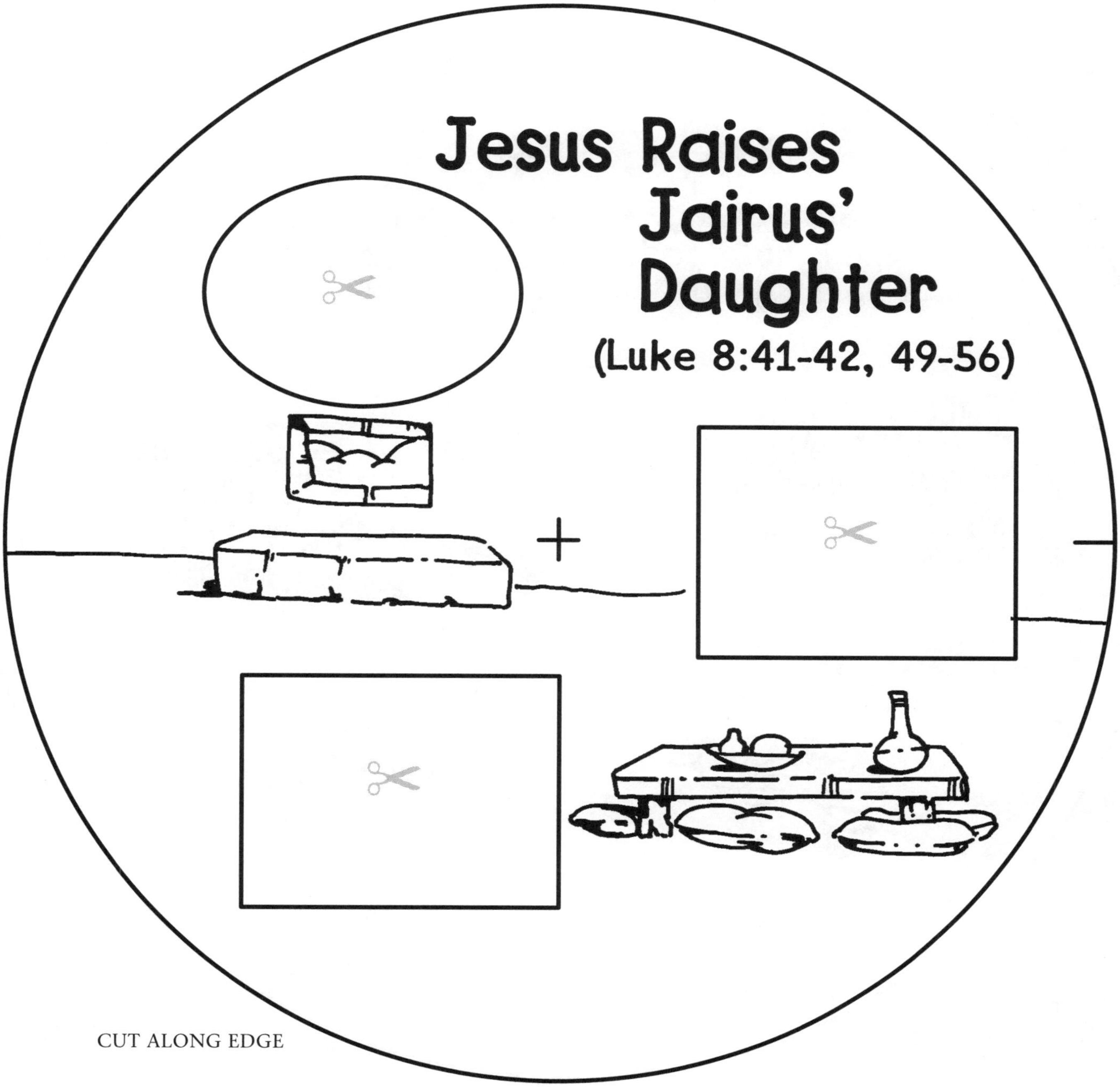
Jesus Raises
Jairus'
Daughter
(Luke 8:41-42, 49-56)

CUT ALONG EDGE

Jesus Raises Jairus' Daughter **Bottom**

CUT ALONG EDGE

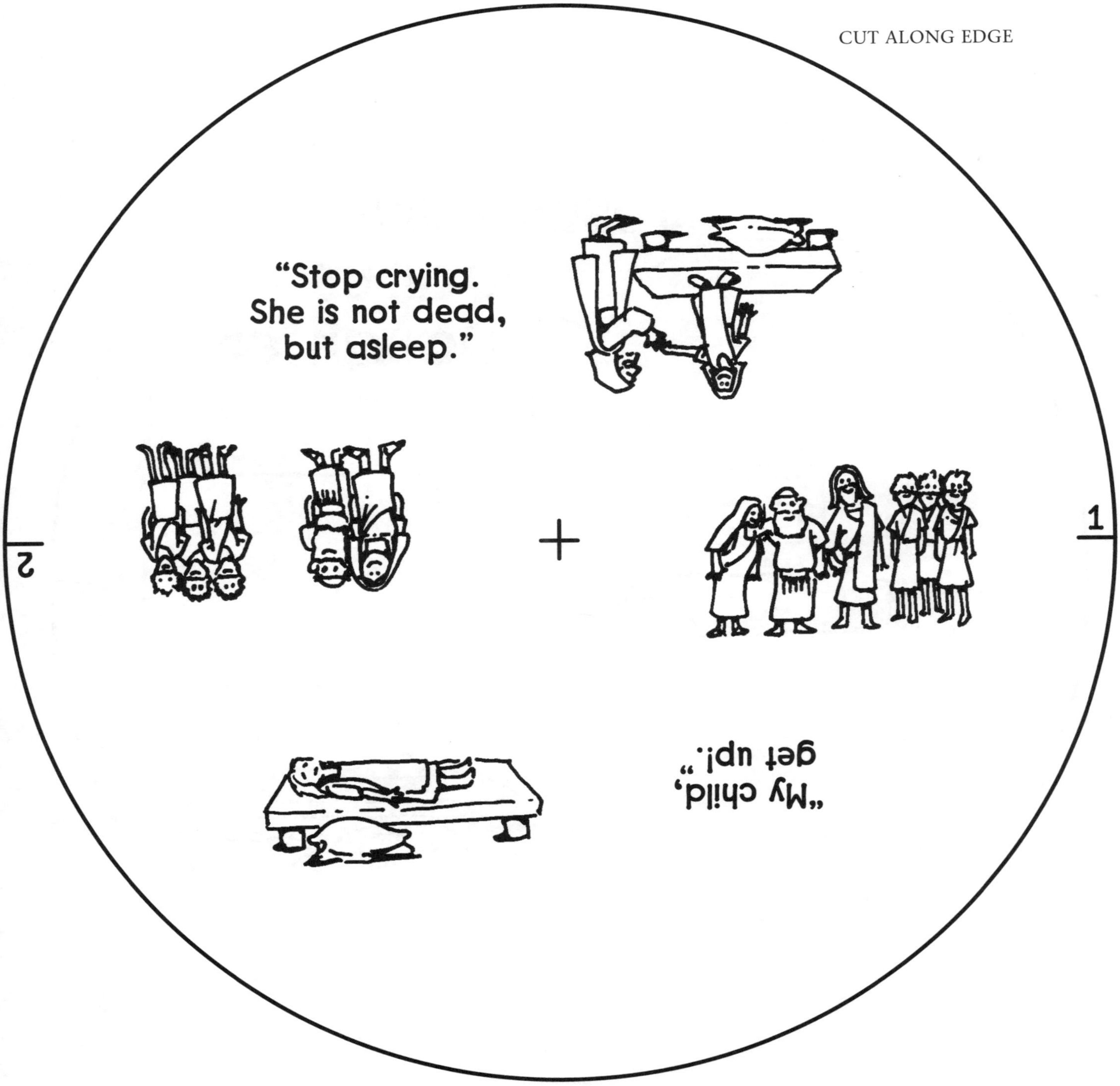
"Stop crying.
She is not dead,
but asleep."
1
2
"My child,
get up!."

Feeding the 5,000

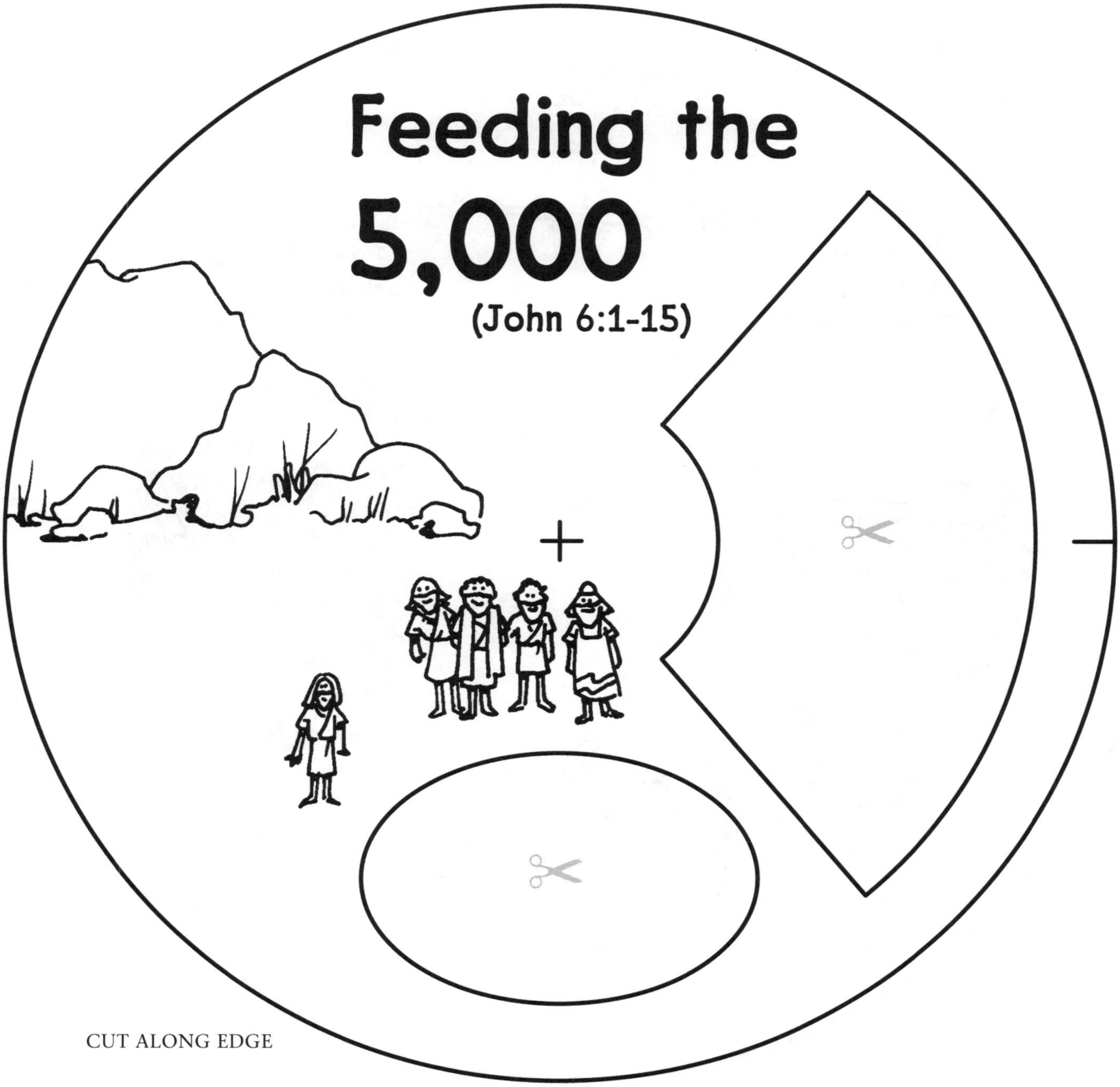
Feeding the
5,000
(John 6:1-15)
CUT ALONG EDGE

Feeding the 5,000

Bottom

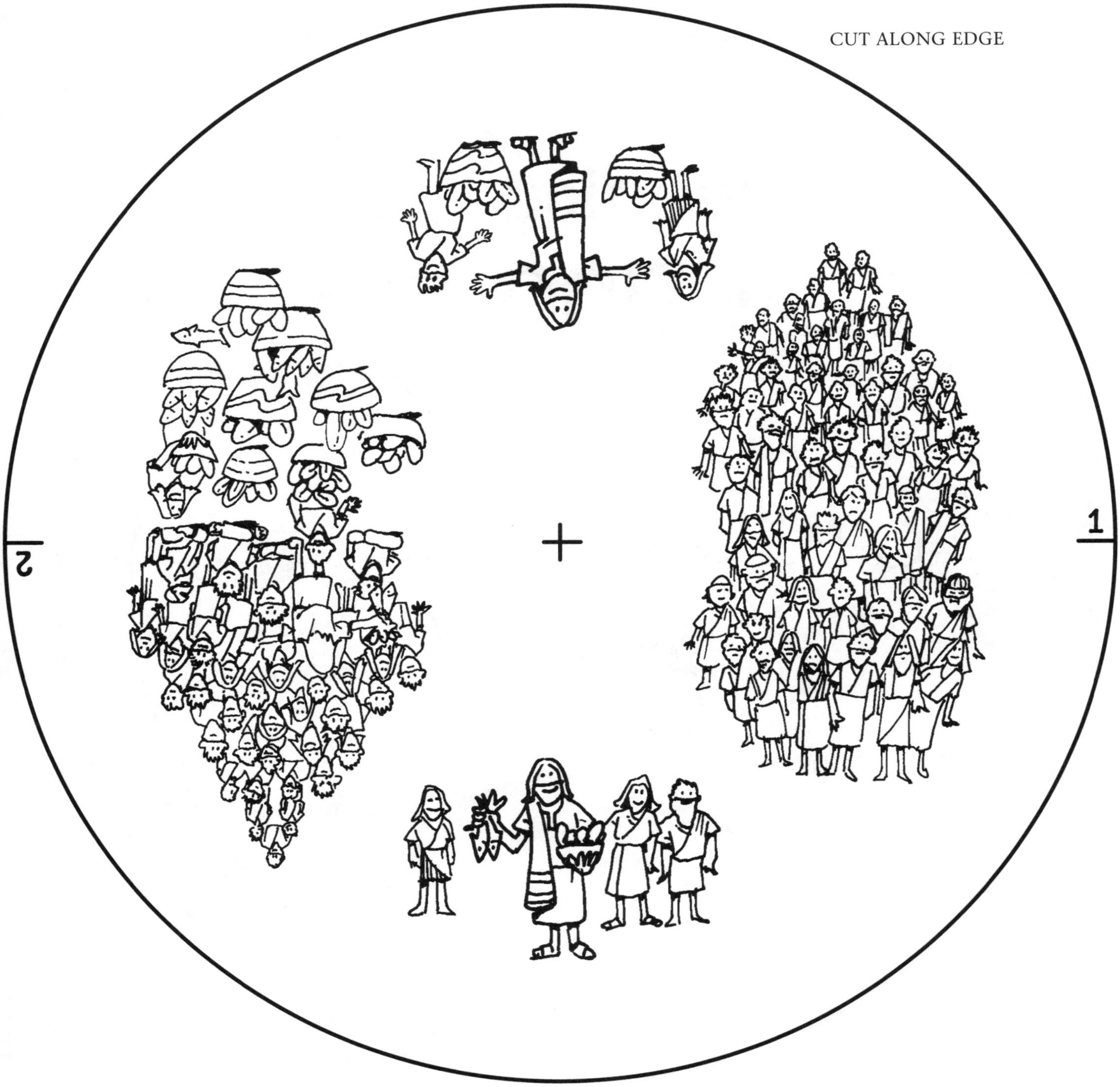

CUT ALONG EDGE
1
2

Jesus & the Children

Jesus &
the Children
(Luke 18:15-17)
CUT ALONG EDGE

Jesus & the Children

Bottom

CUT ALONG EDGE

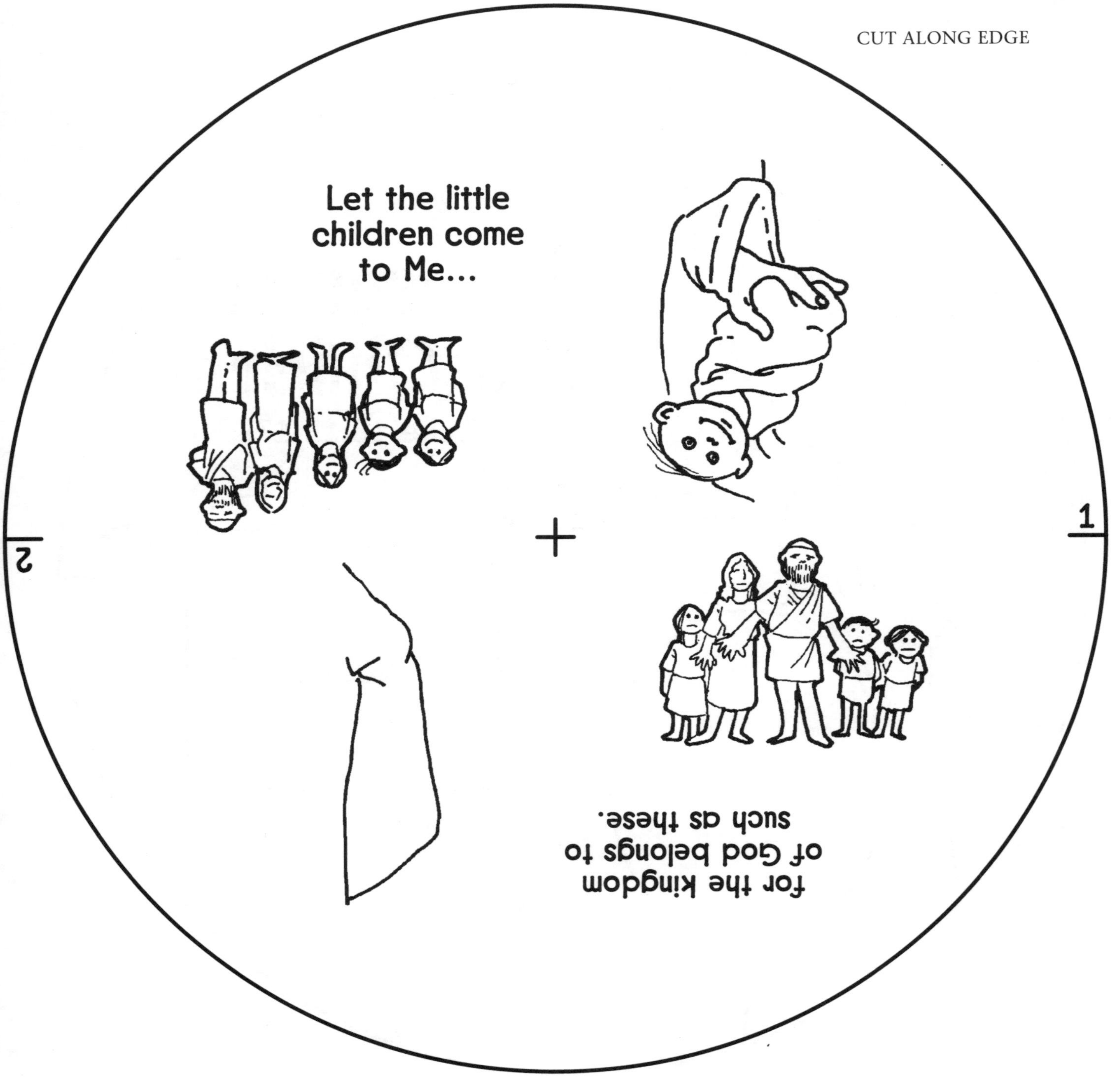
Let the little children come to Me...
for the kingdom of God belongs to such as these.
1
2

Top

The Ten Lepers

The
Ten Lepers
(Luke 17:11-19)
CUT ALONG EDGE

The Ten Lepers

Bottom

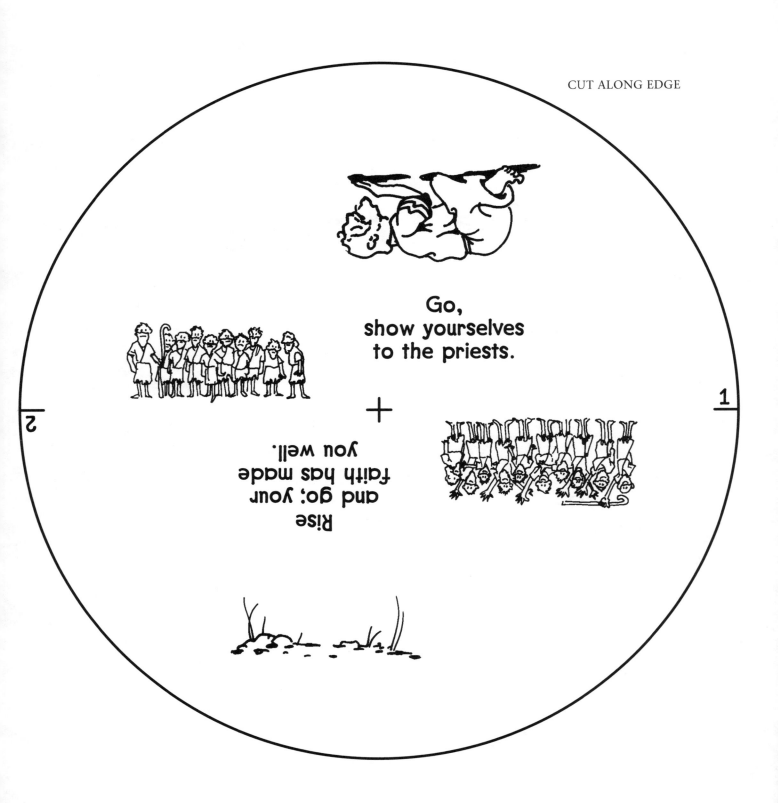

CUT ALONG EDGE

Go,
show yourselves
to the priests.

1

2

Rise
and go; your
faith has made
you well.

Zacchaeus

Zacchaeus
(Luke 19:1-10)

CUT ALONG EDGE

CUT ALONG EDGE

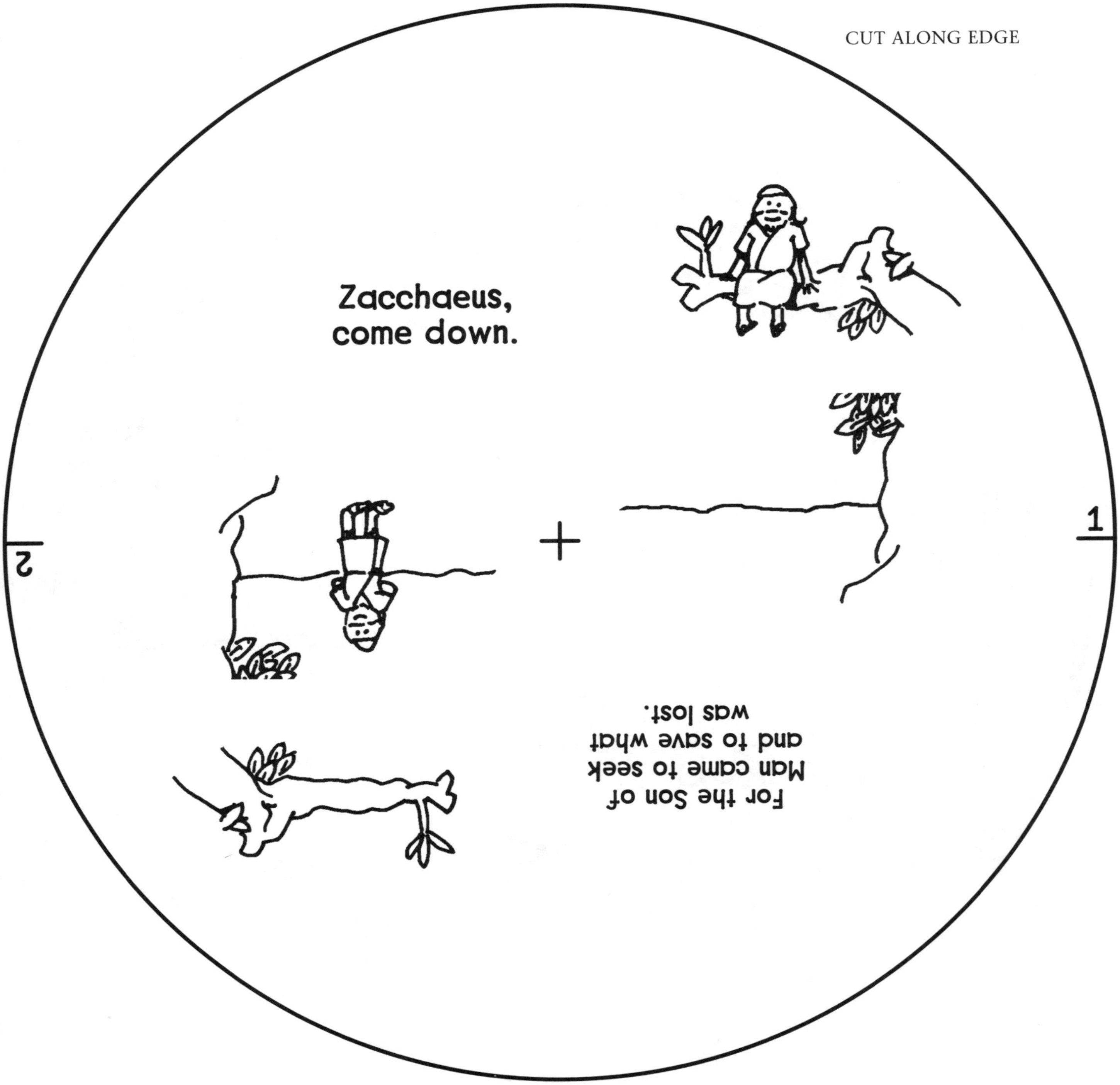
Zacchaeus,
come down.
1
2
For the Son of
Man came to seek
and to save what
was lost.

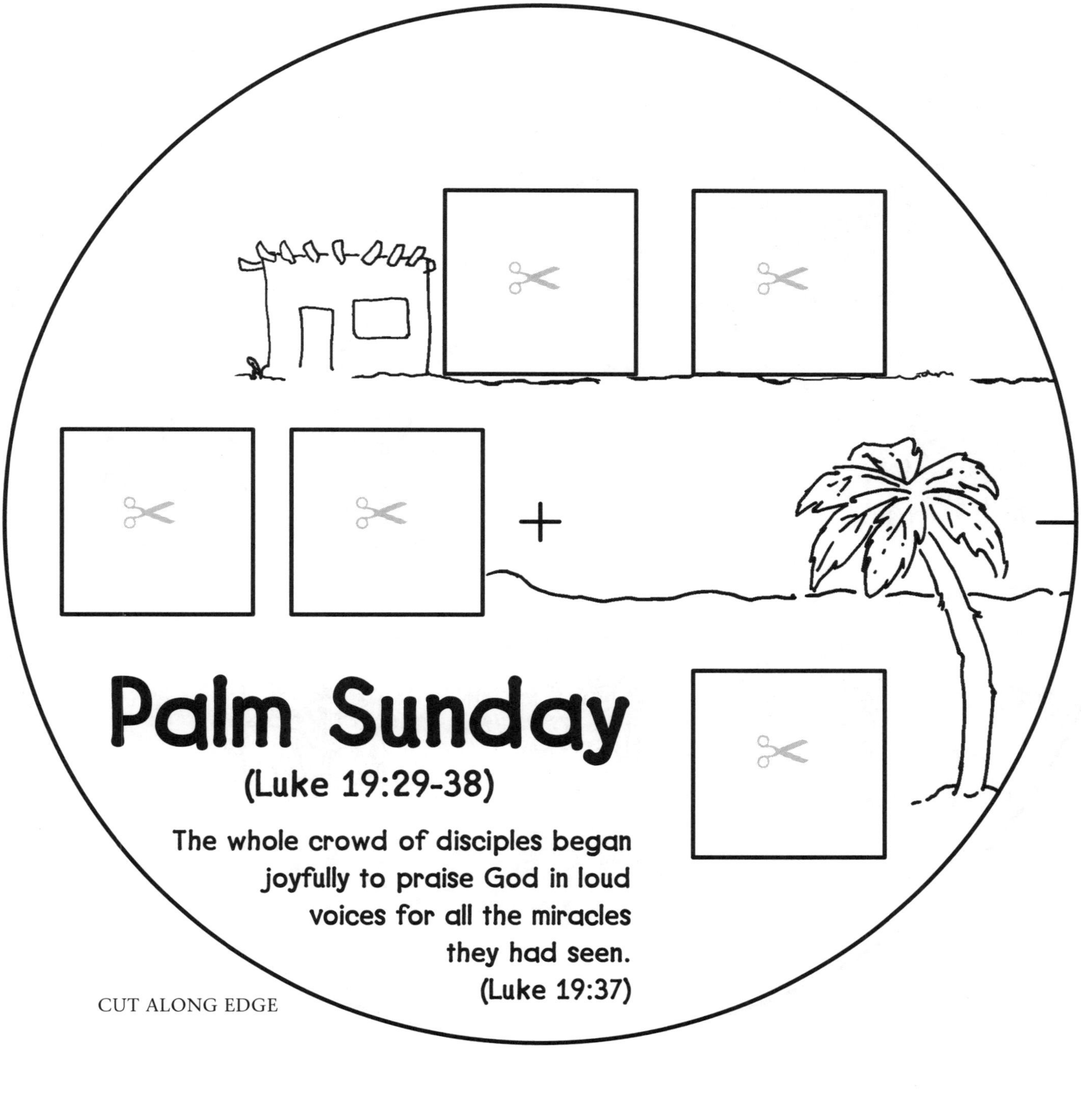
Palm Sunday
(Luke 19:29-38)
The whole crowd of disciples began joyfully to praise God in loud voices for all the miracles they had seen.
(Luke 19:37)
CUT ALONG EDGE

Palm Sunday

Bottom

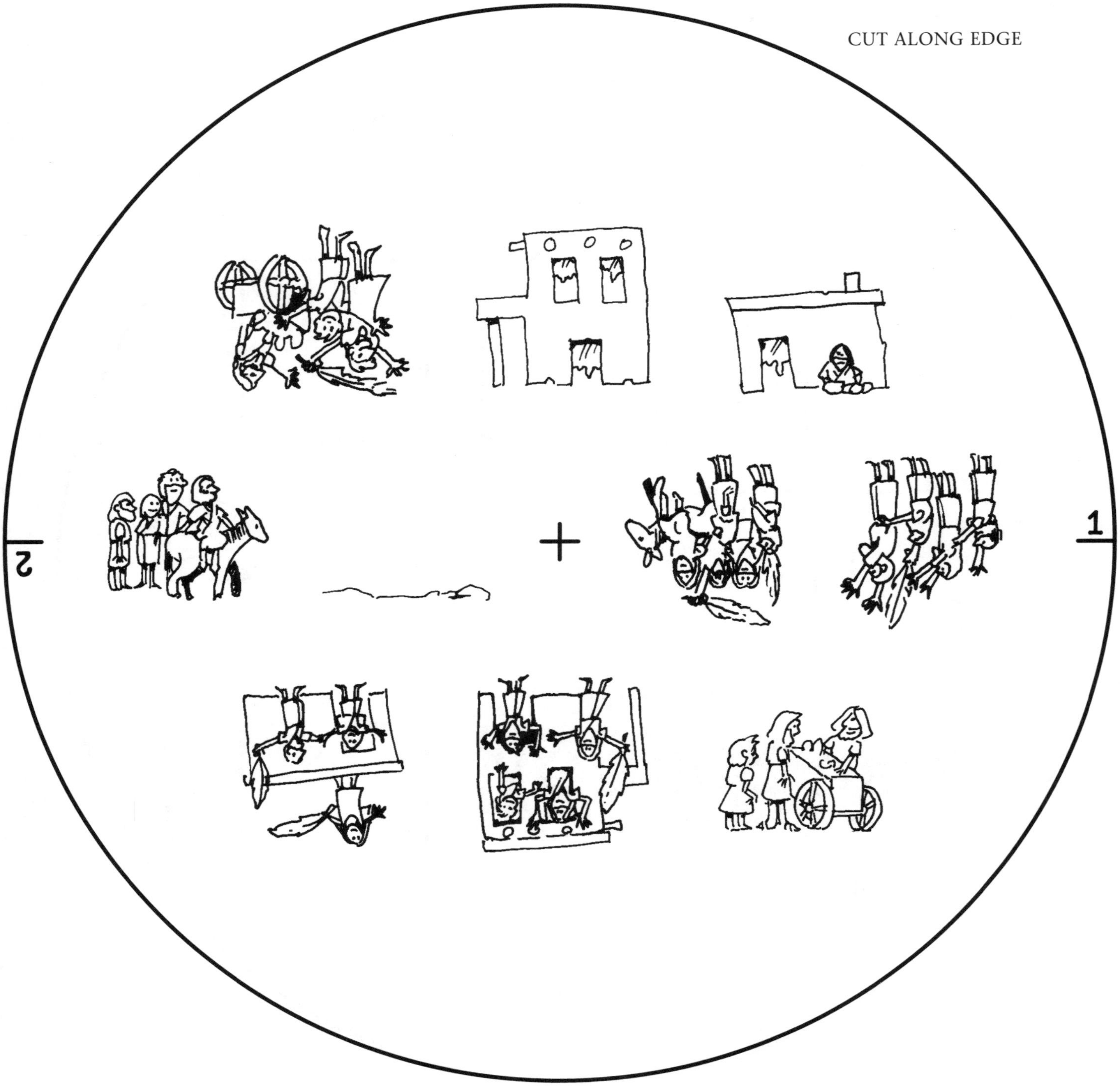
CUT ALONG EDGE
1
2

Top

Jesus Is Crucified

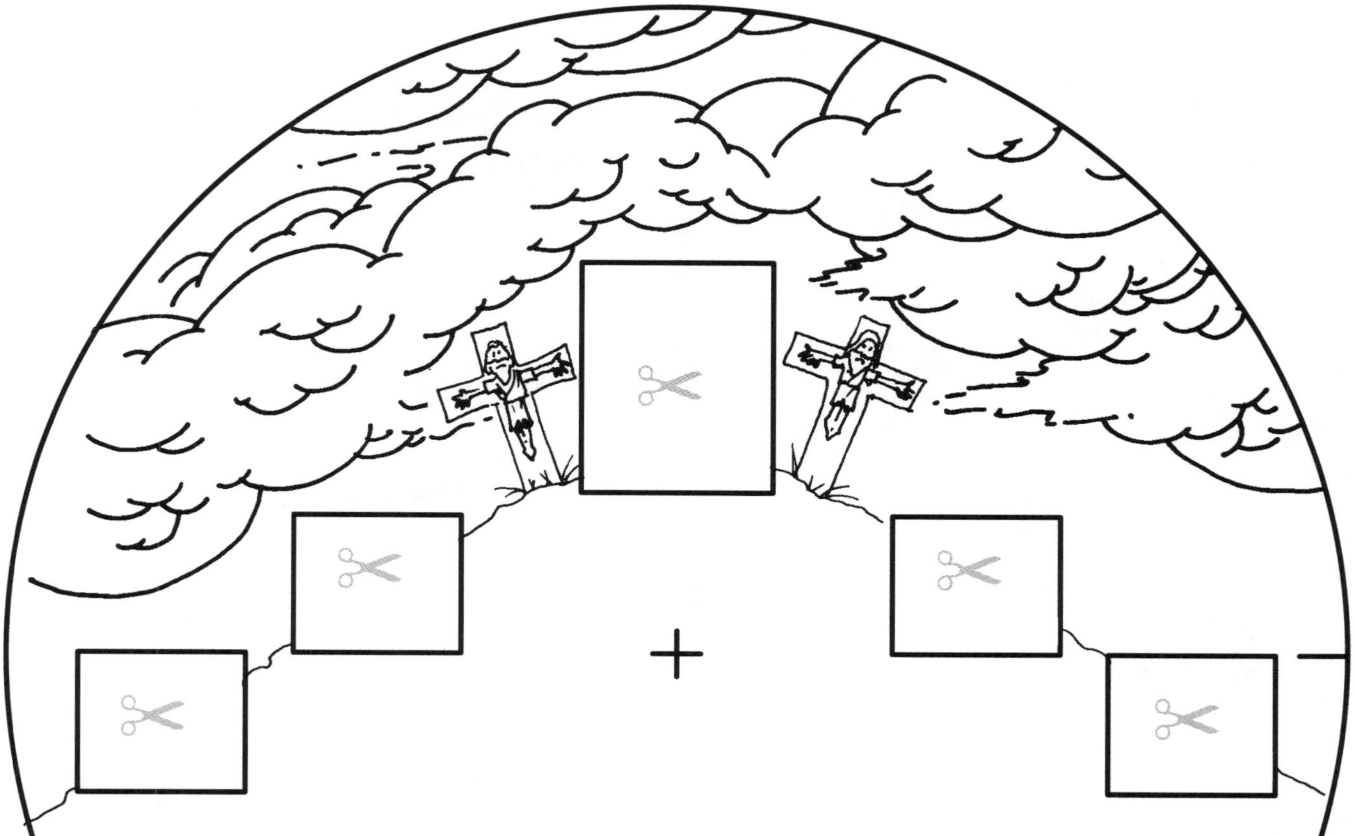

Jesus Is Crucified

(John 19:16-42)

So the soldiers took charge of Jesus.
Carrying His own cross, He went out to the
place of the Skull. Here they crucified Him,
and with Him two others.
John 19:17

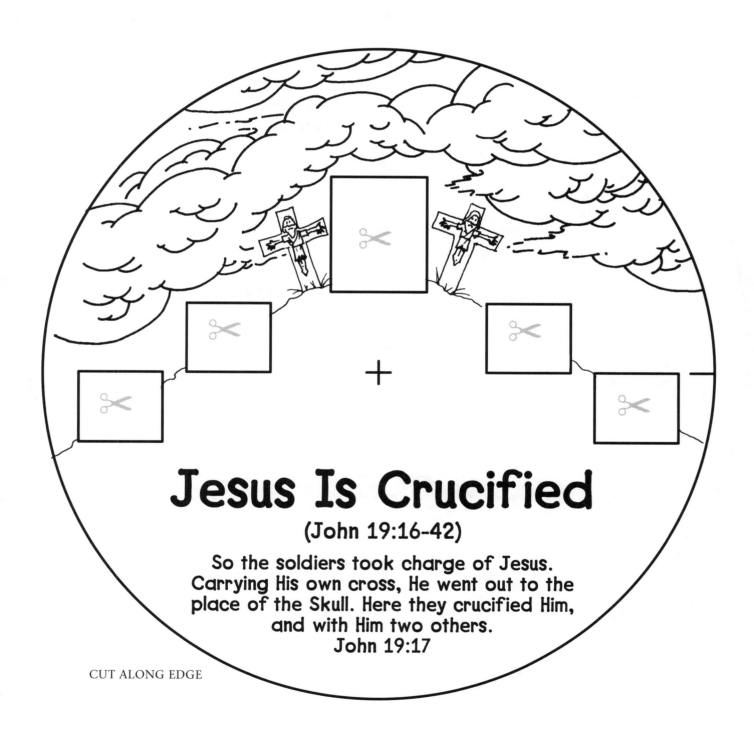

CUT ALONG EDGE

Jesus Is Crucified

Bottom

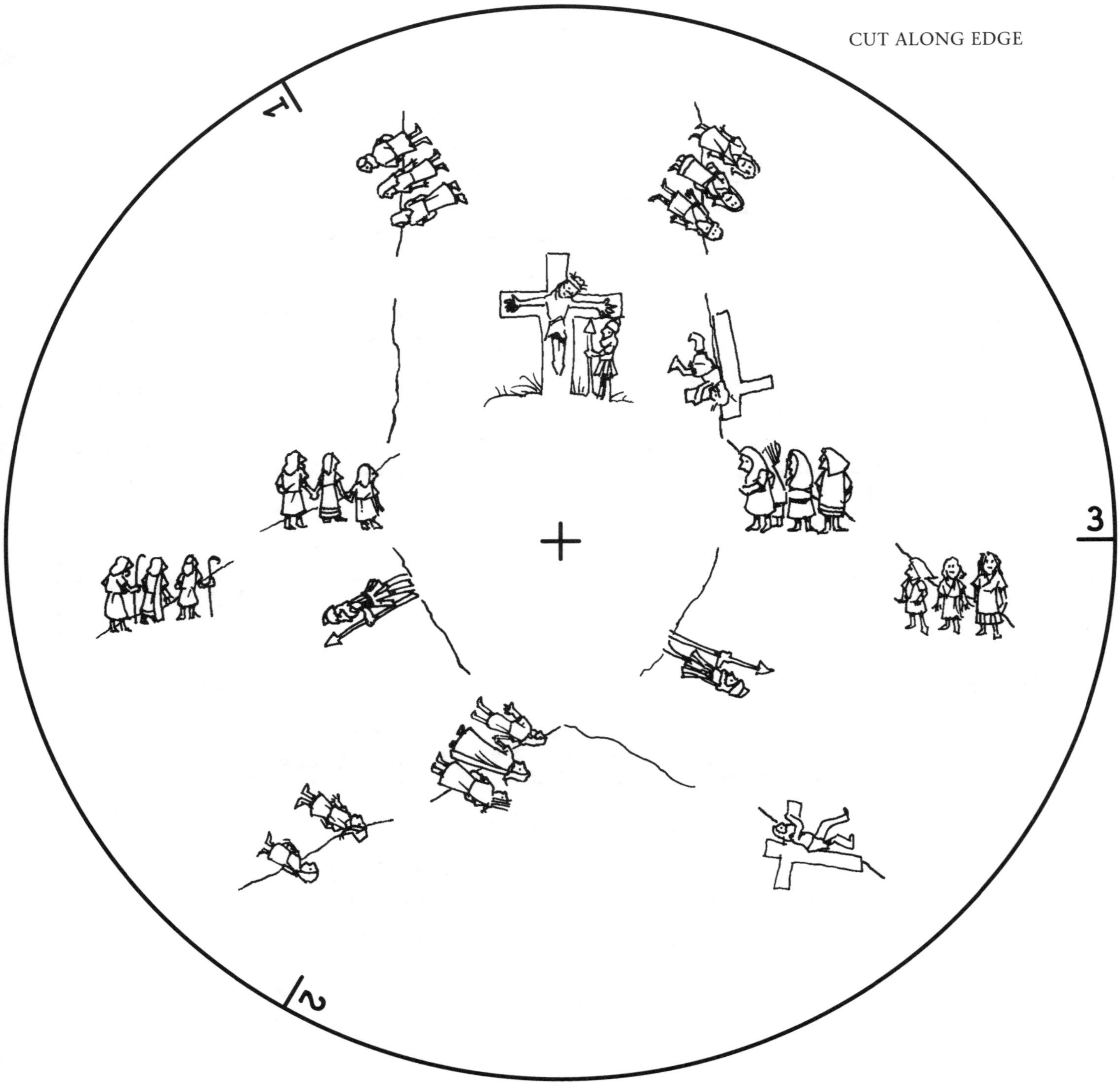
CUT ALONG EDGE
1
2
3

Top

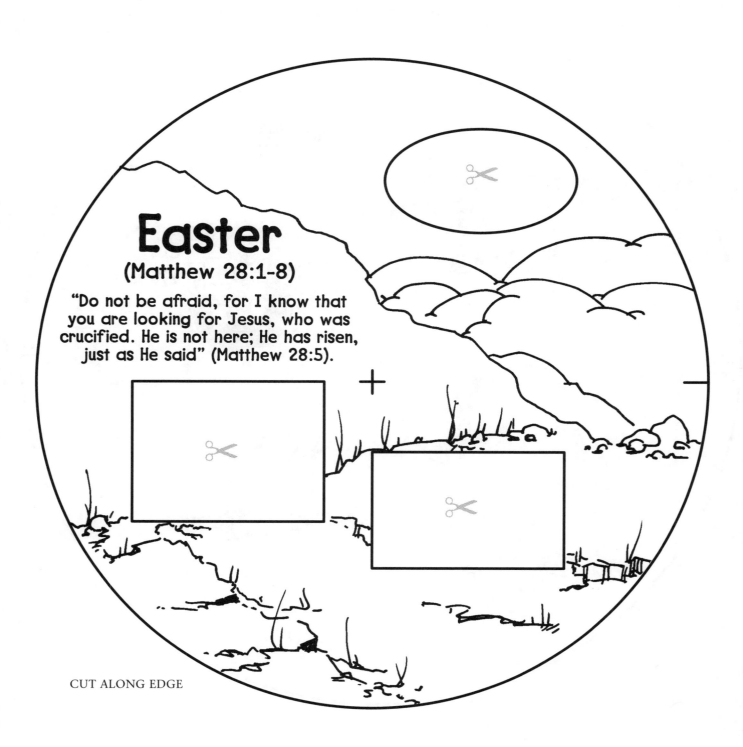

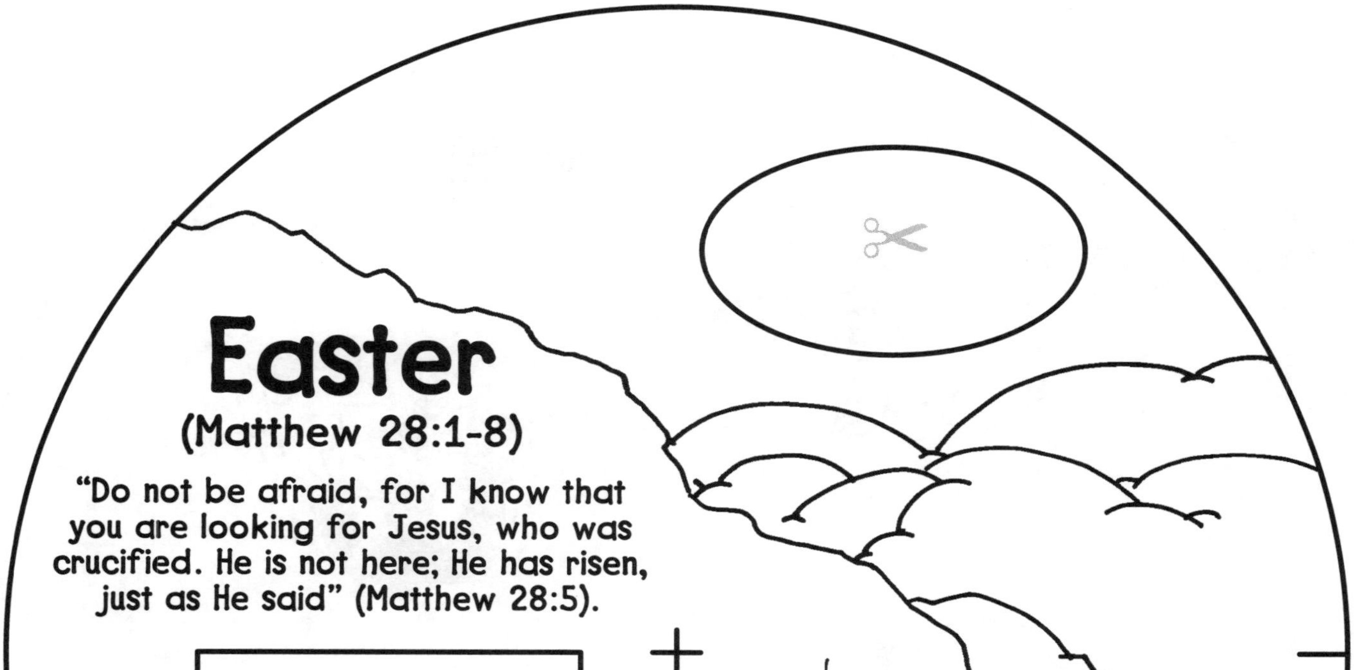
Easter
(Matthew 28:1-8)
"Do not be afraid, for I know that you are looking for Jesus, who was crucified. He is not here; He has risen, just as He said" (Matthew 28:5).
CUT ALONG EDGE

Easter

Bottom

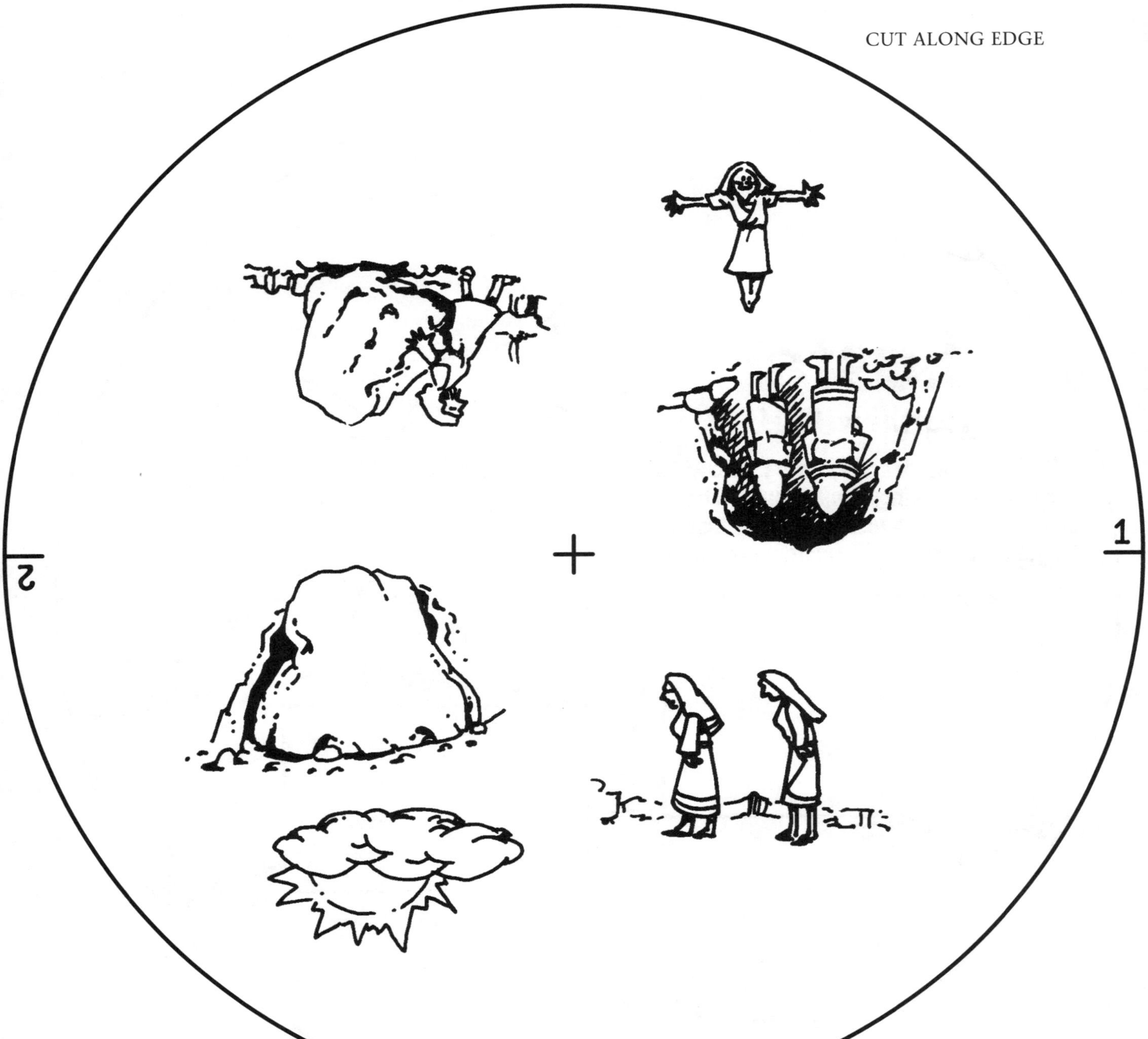
CUT ALONG EDGE
1
2

Top

Breakfast at the Lake

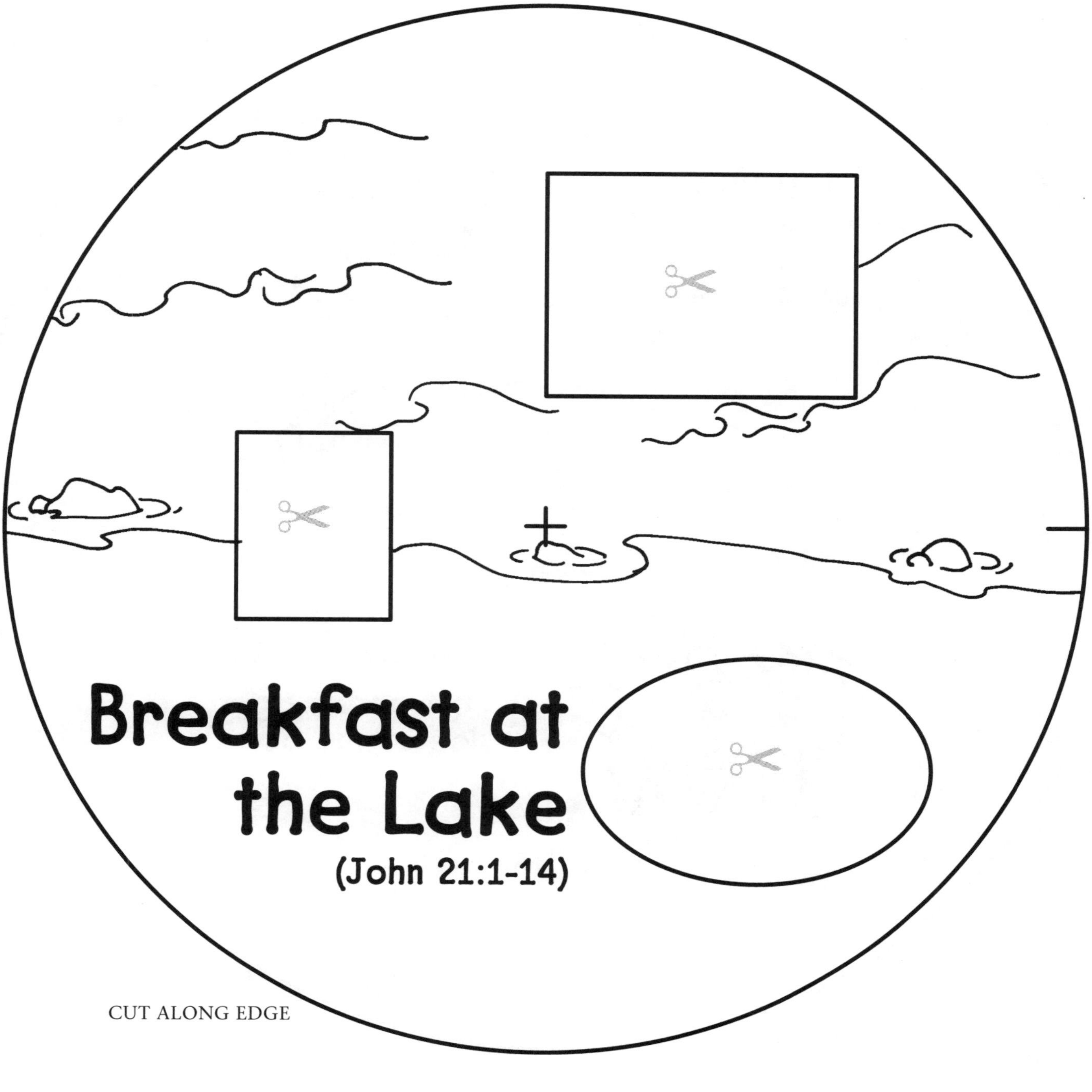
Breakfast at the Lake
(John 21:1-14)

CUT ALONG EDGE

Breakfast at the Lake

Bottom

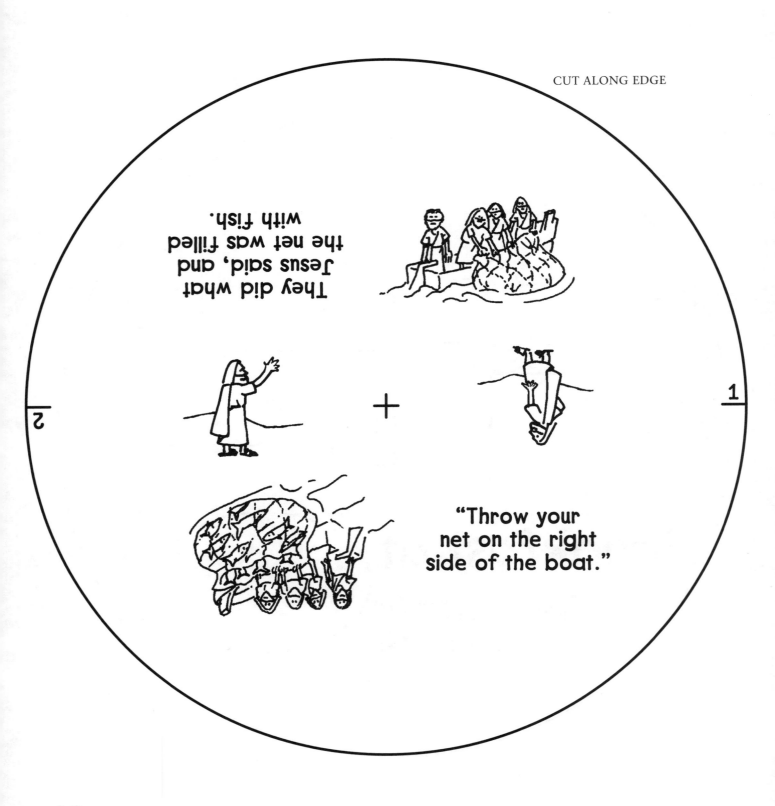

CUT ALONG EDGE

They did what
Jesus said, and
the net was filled
with fish.

2

1

"Throw your
net on the right
side of the boat."

Top

Jesus' Ascension into Heaven

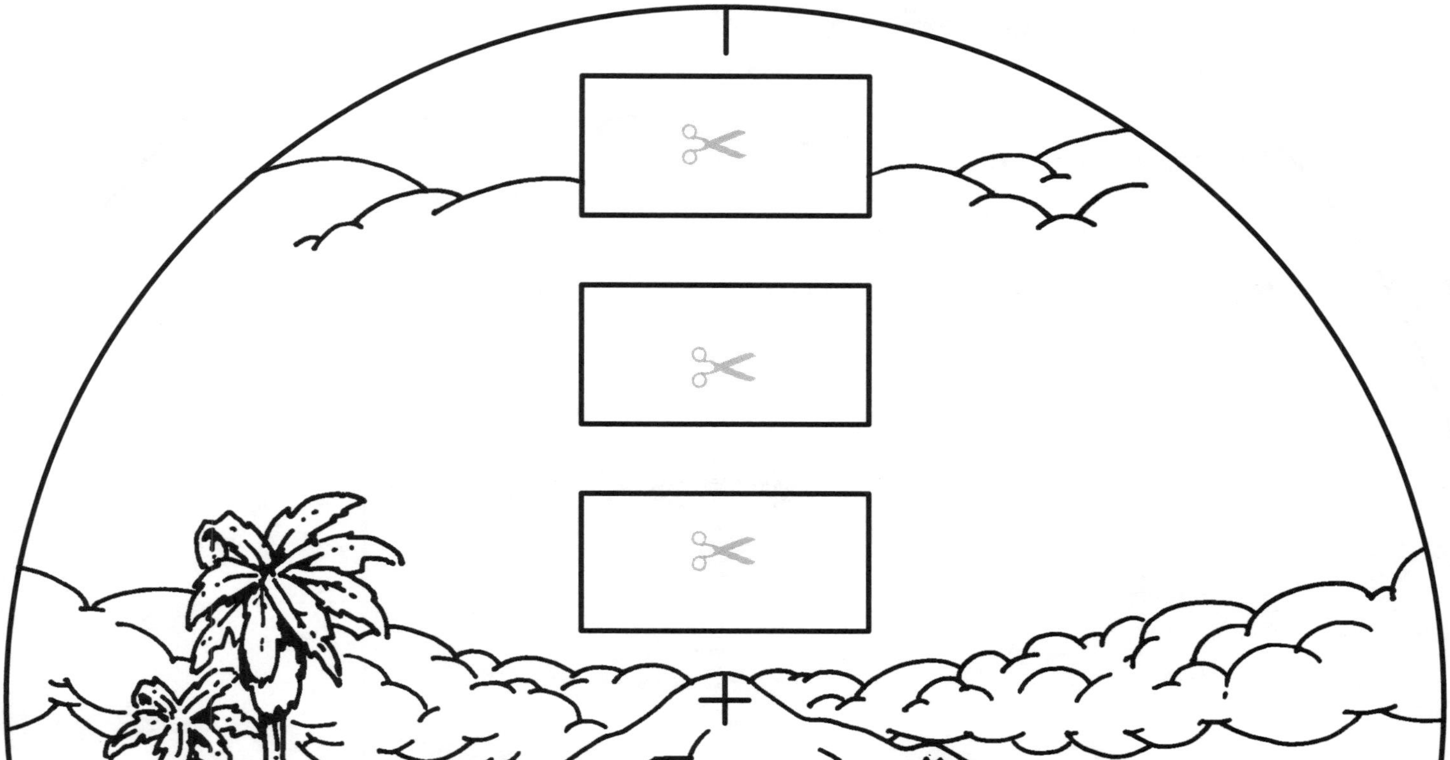
Jesus' Ascension
into Heaven
(Luke 24:50-52)

CUT ALONG EDGE

Jesus' Ascension into Heaven **Bottom**

CUT ALONG EDGE

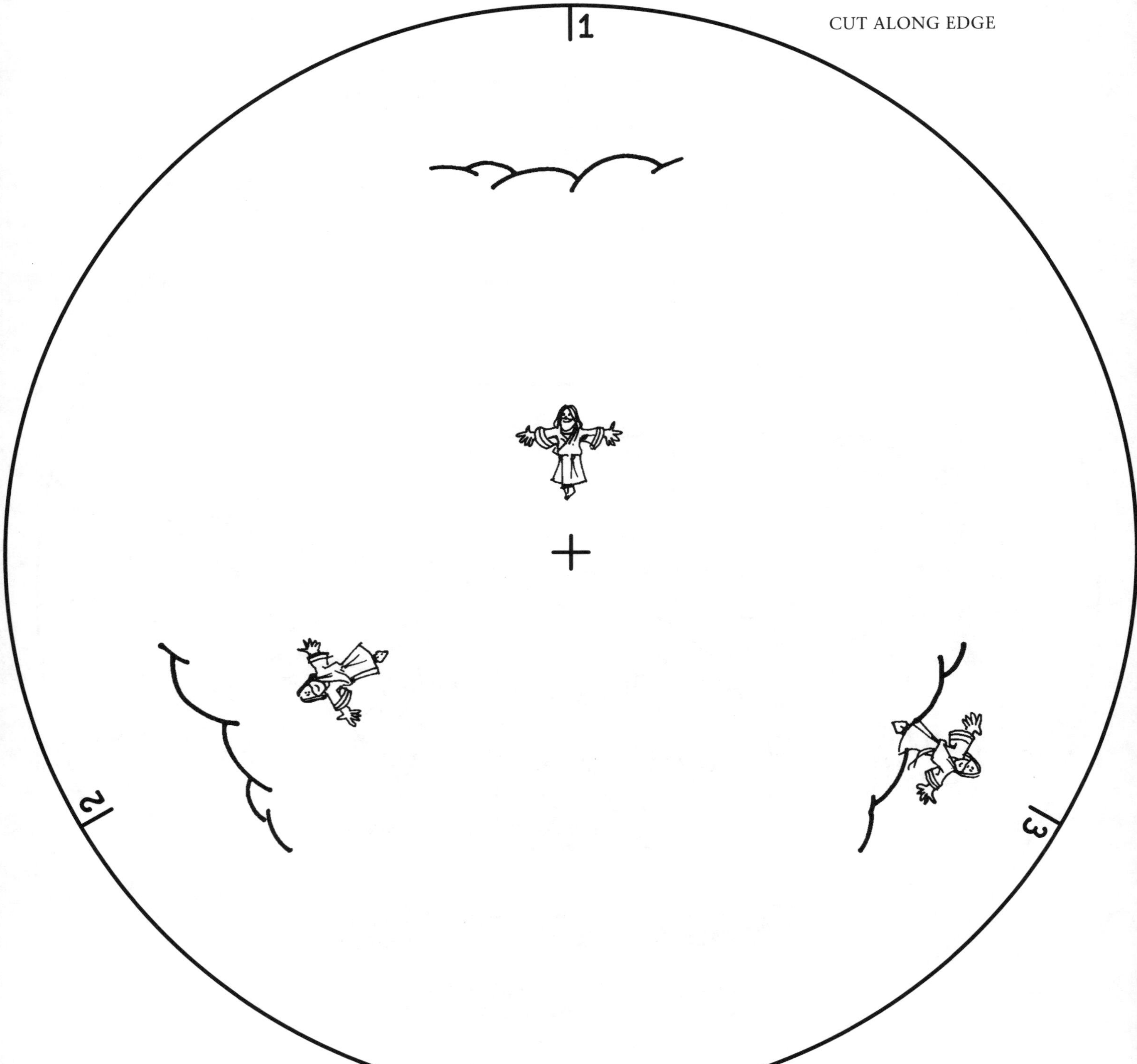
1
2
3

Pentecost

(Acts 2:1-12)

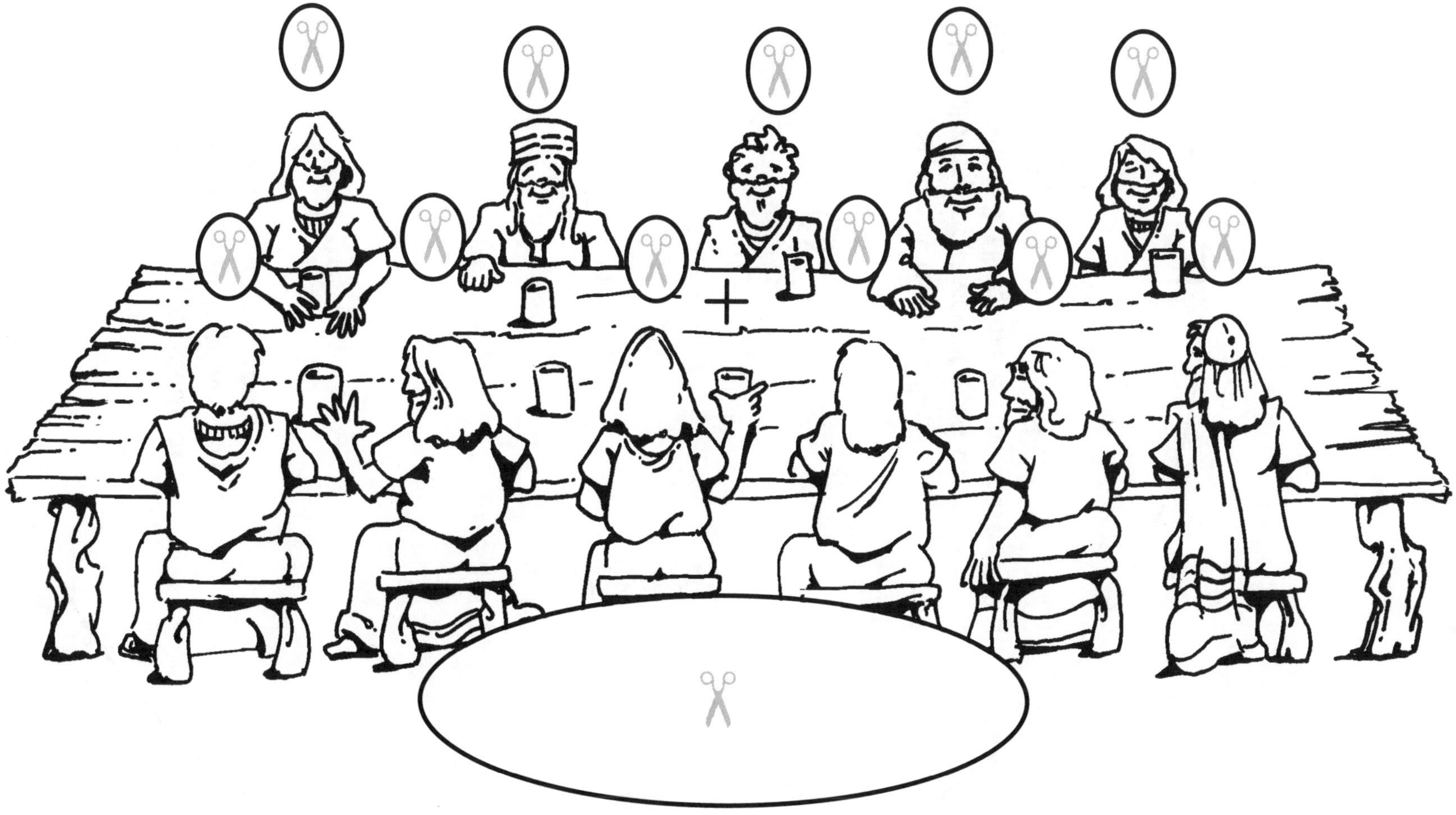

CUT ALONG EDGE

Pentecost

Bottom

CUT ALONG EDGE

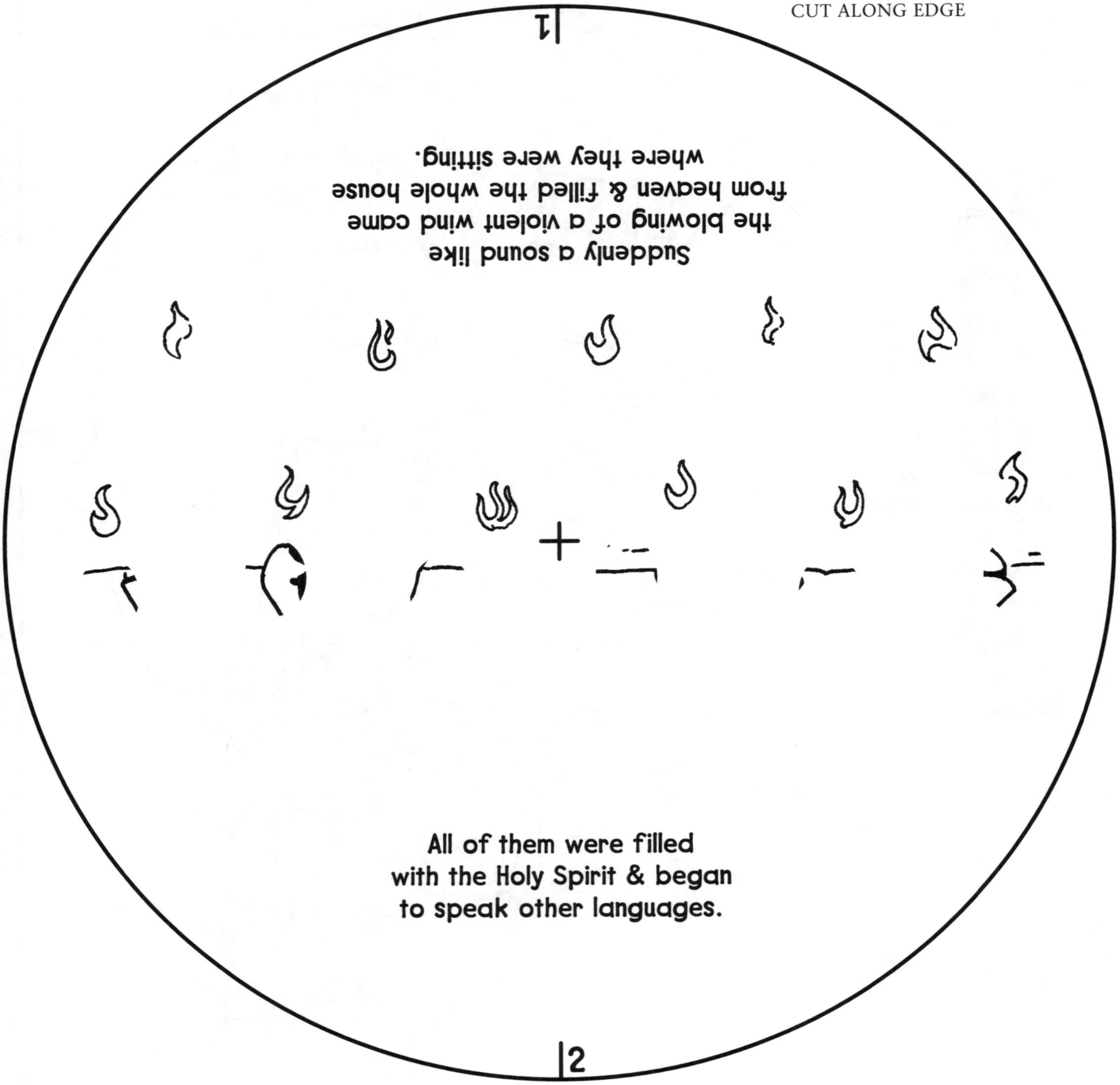
1
Suddenly a sound like
the blowing of a violent wind came
from heaven & filled the whole house
where they were sitting.
All of them were filled
with the Holy Spirit & began
to speak other languages.
2